MACMILLAN MASTER GU

D0268525

General Editor: James Gibson
Published:

Also published by Macmillan

MASTERING ENGLISH LITERATURE R. Gill
MASTERING ENGLISH LANGUAGE S. H. Burton
MASTERING ENGLISH GRAMMAR S. H. Burton

WORK OUT SERIES
WORK OUT ENGLISH LANGUAGE ('O' level and GCSE) S. H. Burton
WORK OUT ENGLISH LITERATURE ('A' level) S. H. Burton

MACMILLAN MASTER GUIDES
THE RIVALS
BY RICHARD SHERIDAN

JEREMY ROWE

MACMILLAN

© Jeremy Rowe 1986

First edition 1986

Published by
MACMILLAN EDUCATION LTD
Houndmills, Basingstoke, Hampshire RG21 2XS
and London
Companies and representatives
throughout the world

Typeset by
TecSet Ltd, Sutton, Surrey
Printed in Hong Kong

British Library Cataloguing in Publication Data
Rowe, Jeremy
The rivals by Richard Sheridan. — (Macmillan
master guides)
1. Sheridan, Richard Brinsley. Rivals, The
I. Title   II. Sheridan, Richard Brinsley. Rivals
822'.6   PR3682.R6
ISBN 0-333-37204-2 Pbk
ISBN 0-333-39466-6 Pbk export

CONTENTS

GENERAL EDITOR'S PREFACE

The aim of the Macmillan Master Guides is to help you to appreciate the book you are studying by providing information about it and by suggesting ways of reading and thinking about it which will lead to a fuller understanding. The section on the writer's life and background has been designed to illustrate those aspects of the writer's life which have influenced the work, and to place it in its personal and literary context. The summaries and critical commentary are of special importance in that each brief summary of the action is followed by an examination of the significant critical points. The space which might have been given to repetitive explanatory notes has been devoted to a detailed analysis of the kind of passage which might confront you in an examination. Literary criticism is concerned with both the broader aspects of the work being studied and with its detail. The ideas which meet us in reading a great work of literature, and their relevance to us today, are an essential part of our study, and our Guides look at the thought of their subject in some detail. But just as essential is the craft with which the writer has constructed his work of art, and this is considered under several technical headings — characterisation, language, style and stage-craft.

The authors of these Guides are all teachers and writers of wide experience, and they have chosen to write about books they admire and know well in the belief that they can communicate their admiration to you. But you yourself must read and know intimately the book you are studying. No one can do that for you. You should see this book as a lamp-post. Use it to shed light, not to lean against. If you know your text and know what it is saying about life, and how it says it, then you will enjoy it, and there is no better way of passing an examination in literature.

JAMES GIBSON

ACKNOWLEDGEMENTS

I wish to thank all those concerned with *The Rivals* when I directed the play at the DePaul/Goodman School of Drama in Chicago in 1982. Their insights have contributed greatly to this Master Guide.

JEREMY ROWE

1 LIFE AND BACKGROUND

1.1 Life

Like other playwrights whose names are inseparable from English comedy, such as William Congreve, George Farquhar and Oscar Wilde, Richard Brinsley Sheridan in fact came from Irish stock. His grandfather, Thomas, was a Doctor of Divinity and a friend of Dean Swift, who wrote *Gulliver's Travels*. Although not rich, Thomas aimed at a gentle, even noble way of life for his household, and the rectory where he lived was in his eyes a veritable mansion; he passed on this ambition for gentility to succeeding generations. Swift said of his friend, with whom he enjoyed a quarrelsome if jocular relationship, that he was 'a generous, honest, good-natured man, but that his perpetual want of discretion and judgement made him act as if he were neither generous, honest nor good-natured'. He could have made the same remark about his godson, Richard's father who was also called Thomas, and just as appropriately about Richard himself.

Richard was born in Dublin on 6 September 1751. The talents and accomplishments of both his parents were of a theatrical nature. His father was in his day a well-known actor, and at the beginning of his career seemed set to rival David Garrick, the leading English actor of the age. One critic applauded him with the comment that 'Hamlet was a character often attempted, but never tolerably by any but Sheridan' - high praise indeed, while Richard, an incisive critic of everything his father attempted, once wrote of his acting in the scene with Hubert in William Shakespeare's *King John* that 'here was a masterpiece of the art'. Unfortunately, Thomas's becoming acting manager of the Theatre Royal, Smock Alley, Dublin in 1745 was a promotion to disaster. Being a man with high ideals and theatrical principles, he immediately set about reforming the theatre which, as he saw it, had fallen into a moral and artistic decline. However, neither his audience nor his actors were the slightest bit interested in reform, and after ten years of fretful rule, Thomas found himself the cause and the object of a series of riots sparked off by anti-English sentiments provoked by a particularly colonial play currently in the Smock Alley repertoire. The theatre was pillaged and wrecked, and the Sheridan family was forced to flee ignominiously to England.

From that time on, Thomas was to have an uneven career. His reputation secured him some large roles, but his acting style was of the old, declamatory kind, and his popularity could not compete with that of Garrick, whose performances were so much more brilliantly lifelike. From time to time he put on a play in Ireland, and he wrote treatises on elocution and education. Much of his spare time was spent battling with his son, Richard.

Frances Sheridan, Richard's mother, was a writer. Her play, *The Discovery*, in which Garrick gave one of his highly successful comic performances, received the seal of his approval: 'It is,' he said, 'one of the best comedies I have ever read.' One descriptive and evocative phrase concerning Mrs Sheridan has come down to us from Dr Parr, one of Richard's teachers. While he found the father 'a wrong-headed, whimsical man', he found the mother 'quite celestial'. Separation from such a mother during long stretches of his childhood inevitably affected Richard's development and character.

Many artists display signs of genius at an early age; not so Sheridan. Sir Winston Churchill made no great mark at Harrow, the famous public school, nor did our author. Harrow had always been, like Eton, a school for the rich, for aristocrats, for future politicians, but also for scholars; but before he even arrived there, Richard had been proclaimed by his schoolmaster 'an impenetrable dunce', and his academic results at Harrow supported this verdict. There were reasons for his lack of success that had little to do with innate ability. He was unhappy away from his brother Charles and his sisters Elizabeth and Alicia, and particularly wretched in his absence from his mother. In 1762, they had fled with his father to France, in order to escape the disgrace of bankruptcy. Then too, the atmosphere of the school was foreign to him; he did not make friends, he spent much of his time alone, he indulged in poetry and practical jokes as if they were alternative ways of escaping from the school routine. Above all, he felt out of place as a player's son, all the more so because his lack of money was evident and yet he clearly had pretensions to the status of a gentleman.

All his life Sheridan was to be dogged by the desire to rise above the middle rank. Ironically, it was the theatre which first offered him the means to rise, yet the theatre was to become the domain from which he felt compelled to escape in order to fulfil his social image of himself: an image that began with the ambitious twinkle in his grandfather's eye, but which was strengthened by these insecurities of his school days. Dr Parr was the one teacher who took a real interest in the boy, but he did not arrive at Harrow until Richard had been there for five years. He perceived the remarkable talents of the future writer, but said that he could find no way of drawing them out. Sheridan was charming, good-looking, well-mannered, inclined to melancholy, and frequently mischievous. Although he was not much good at Latin, he was obviously clever, and, like many another schoolboy, where he was irritating he was also apt to be endearing. One suspects that it was at Harrow that he learned to take refuge from uncongenial work and surroundings in the comedy of his imagination.

In 1766 Mrs Sheridan died and was buried in France; Richard remained at Harrow three long years after her death. Eventually, however, Thomas returned to England, where he removed Richard from school entirely and took his son's education upon himself. During the experiment, father and son began to get on each other's nerves. On the other hand, it did mean that Richard became skilled in the arts and manners of a London gentleman, particularly in riding and fencing, for he was 'upon the town' a whole year. Then the family moved to Bath, the fashionable spa in the West of England, where Thomas intended to start a new Academy of Oratory; Richard was to assist him. This motherless family must have looked poor and curiously vulnerable among the elegant trappings of Bath, but such a group was bound to meet adventure sooner or later. As it turned out, the adventure was to be the source for *The Rivals*.

Bath was a city rich in literary associations, social opportunities, character types and beautiful women. At first Sheridan seems to have been a little wary of the delights it had to offer, with its new Assembly Rooms and ceremonious dances and its wealth of intrigue, but he compensated for this shyness by writing. His first creation was a series of burlesques, comic literary imitations and dramatic sketches, written with an old friend from Harrow, Nathaniel Halhed. Their success was purely local, but it spurred them on to more ambitious endeavours and they managed to find a publisher for their translation of *The Love Epistles of Aristaenetus*, a fifth-century Greek poet whose works were wildly fanciful. It was not long, however, before these strivings towards poetic glory were temporarily deflected, and the study of books gave way to the study of a certain young lady. It was, perhaps, unfortunate that it was the same young lady who attracted both of them.

Miss Elizabeth Linley, commonly called Eliza by family and friends, was beautiful. She was also famous among the higher echelons of Bath society for her singing; and since a disappointed suitor had, with extraordinary gallantry, given her three thousand pounds (almost £100 000 in today's money) after she refused him, her charms were supplemented by an attractive dowry. In our age, such a mercenary consideration might seem to have little to do with love. In the eighteenth century, as *The*

Rivals makes clear, inherited money was often necessary for the success of a marriage.

Richard Sheridan was by no means the only young man to surrender to Miss Linley's charms; indeed, he kept his own passion a secret while listening sympathetically as others praised her adoringly; among these confidants, as well as Nathaniel Halhed, was his own brother, Charles. A third suitor, but one who did not seek Richard's counsel, was Captain Matthews; his suit was more menacing than youthful romance, for Captain Matthews was a married man. His importunate attentions eventually forced Miss Linley to look around for a knight in shining armour to call to her rescue; from our vantage point, her choice seems predestined.

In 1772 Richard helped Eliza to avoid the Captain's advances by escorting her to France, where she was to take refuge in a convent until she could be assured of peace on her return. The heady atmosphere of the elopement was no doubt partly responsible for their being privately married by a Catholic priest near Calais; such a hasty decision lacked prudence, and indeed because the couple were under age and could not be married without their parents' consent, their marriage was invalid according to law; but then law was probably not Eliza's strong point, any more than it is that of Lydia Languish.

After the ceremony, the fugitive couple continued on to Lille where the convent was, and there all the excitement took its toll; Eliza fell ill. After residing with the nuns for a few days, she was moved to the house of a certain Dr Dolman. Richard stayed in a hotel, where he had the thankless task of writing home to explain the situation to Eliza's family and his own.

Bath, that cauldron of gossip, was seething with rumours, and there was a large faction inclined to think Sheridan a greater villain than Matthews; the press followed the story eagerly; as may be imagined, the Linley family was in a state of concern and outrage. Something had to be done. Eliza was engaged to sing in the oratorio season to which the theatres were dedicated each Lent, a time of penance in the Christian calendar when more colourful entertainments were deemed inappropriate. With characteristic practicality, her father went to Lille to fetch Eliza back; as a director of music, he could not allow his daughter to renege on a contract, elopement or not. Once he had arrived in Lille and had heard the whole story, his temper subsided under the illusion that the affair would die a natural death once Eliza became involved in her engagement at Covent Garden and Richard returned to Bath. This was a flawed hope from the start, for our hero had no intention of returning to Bath. His adversary, Matthews, was biding his time in London, after having slandered Sheridan to all and sundry in Bath and libelled him in the newspapers; Richard's heightened sense of honour would not allow the matter to rest without a public apology or, failing that, a duel. What took place in Hyde Park on the evening of May 4th could not be accurately described as a duel; it was more of a chase with weapons, and not a little farcical; however, Matthews was humiliated and disarmed, and with the worst possible grace gave the apology for his conduct that Sheridan demanded.

Sheridan then hurried back to Bath in cloak and dagger style, leaving rumour to carry the news of his victory to the ears of his beloved. Sheepishly, Matthews trailed behind, and on arrival found himself shunned by all his acquaintances. He returned to his home in Wales, but found disgrace awaiting him there as well. An Irish gentleman by the name of Mr Barnett, seeing how badly Matthews was treated by his neighbours, decided to take him in hand; he rekindled the sparks of anger in his friend and offered his services as a second, should there be a sequel to the Hyde Park incident. Mr Barnett's role in the real life comedy closely resembles that of Sir Lucius in *The Rivals*.

Given Matthews' disposition and Barnett's ability to play on it, a second duel was bound to occur. Matthews insulted and accused his opponent, and their seconds met to make precise arrangements. The duel took place soon after 3 am on July 1st, 1772. There was nothing funny about this one, and the fighting was rough. Both men were wounded, Sheridan severely. He was dragged to the post-chaise and then taken to a hotel, where his wounds were dressed by the best surgeons in the city. He confessed afterwards that he thought he was dying.

The news of the duel soon reached Thomas Sheridan, who was in London at the time; he flew into a fury, but did not know whether to treat his son as a criminal or a hero. For want of a better reaction, he decided he would refuse to speak to him, while also forbidding him any visits to Eliza or the rest of her family. Mr Linley did not object to this interdict; for one thing, Richard had no money and was therefore an unwelcome suitor for Eliza's hand. Thomas's motives for denying his son access to this young professional singer were snobbish rather than financial; his children were expected to marry into the gentry. At this point of stalemate, Thomas was engaged to act in a play in Dublin, and off he went, banishing Richard to a remote farm owned by friends, where he was to recover from his wounds and resume his studies.

The fruits of love were forbidden, but that only added to their appeal. Correspondence flowed between Richard and his beloved. Elizabeth and Alicia, Richard's sisters, took much delight in assisting the romance. The banished Romeo became increasingly histrionic, and resorted to disguise in order to converse with his Juliet. He dressed up as a coachman and waited for her at the stage door of Covent Garden, and so managed to escort her home. There were whispered vows and tears in profusion. Under all this excess of sensibility, though, there existed a real and growing attachment, and little by little both fathers came to accept the match. There remained the sticky problem of what Richard was to do with his professional life. So that his status might be raised to that of a professional gentleman, he was enrolled at Middle Temple to study law, on April 6th, 1773. Exactly a week later, he and Eliza were married.

Why has it seemed necessary to introduce you to these events? Clearly because in a variety of ways they turn up in *The Rivals*; they furnished the playwright with a plot, a collection of characters and a living satire. Thomas Moore, Sheridan's first biographer and a personal friend, attributed Faulkland with all his nice anxieties to 'self-observation' on the part of his creator, while, according to him, Captain Absolute represents another side of his nature. Similarly, Eliza may be seen as divided into the capricious Lydia and the patient Julia. The relationship depicted between the Absolutes, father and son, must be one of the most autobiographical elements in the play. Some of Captain Matthews found his way into Bob Acres, and, as has been demonstrated, Mr Barnett's role was similar to that of Sir Lucius. Mrs Malaprop's direct ancestors are largely literary, and she owes something to a character created by Frances Sheridan in one of her plays. Nevertheless, she, along with Lucy, Fag and David give the impression of having been picked out from the bustling thoroughfares of Bath and deposited upon the stage.

For a few years Richard's motto could have been a sentence he wrote in a letter to his father: 'The surest way not to fail is to determine to succeed.' He did not see himself succeeding in the law, but he recognised his chance as a writer of plays. By November 1774 *The Rivals* had been completed and was in rehearsal. Sheridan was twenty-three.

After an initial failure on the first night, and subsequent rewriting, the play was a resounding success. In the same year, he wrote the consistently popular operetta, *The Duenna*. In 1776, in partnership with James Ford and Mr Linley, who was still seeking a more stable livelihood for his son-in-law, Sheridan assumed management of the Drury Lane Theatre, taking upon himself the mantle of the great Garrick. His lifestyle soared. He and Eliza began to keep the kind of London household of which generations of Sheridans had dreamt; they entertained on a lavish scale.

In 1777 his greatest comedy, *The School for Scandal*, was produced for the first time, and it was immediately as popular as it has been ever since. Sheridan was firmly established among the celebrities of his age. Yet, before he was thirty, the dramatist's phase of his career was, to all intents and purposes, over. The last of his enduring comedies, *The Critic*, appeared in 1779.

Richard Brinsley Sheridan, with the theatrical world at his feet, became a politician. It is true that he had always longed, like his father, for a gentility that the stage could not provide, but that was not the whole story; nor was the change of direction completely impulsive, for he retained the profitable business operation at the Drury Lane; nor was his decision a sudden one. As early as 1776 he wrote a disputation to counteract Dr Johnson's indictment of the American colonies. One has to conclude that Sheridan truly believed his vocation to be that of a statesman and orator, a supporter of those in search of liberty.

His reputation in the House was mainly as an orator; as one would expect from his background, he was a highly entertaining and colourful speaker. He was a leading member of the Whig party, which traditionally supported the House of Hanover, while the Tory party did its best to keep King and Court in check. The Whigs were tolerant of dissenters from the Church of England and on the whole favoured the status quo in matters of state. It was the party of the great landowners, some of whom had inherited their estates, others of whom had made fortunes in trade and then purchased them.

One of Sheridan's most admired achievements as a politician was his impeachment of Warren Hastings, Governor-General of India, against whose supposed corruption and misuse of power he fulminated eloquently for hours at a stretch on successive occasions, leaving his listeners astounded. He had a resonant voice, the presence of an actor and an unequalled turn of phrase, and was most at home when he could use his gifts to further the cause of justice among peoples. He supported the French Revolution, for instance, when it seemed to provide the answer to the gross inequalities of European society, and he was a constant champion of the Catholic community in Ireland.

He loved causes, but he also loved the game of politics, and this beguiled him into a habit of placing quite heavy bets on the outcome of issues being debated in the House. He had no idea about how to handle money, and these bets no doubt contributed to the financial trouble in which he and his family were to find themselves. Although he did not bite the hand that continued to feed him, that is, the Drury Lane, he certainly borrowed from it. A combination of gambling, drinking, generosity and carelessness led him into debt. It is an irony, though perhaps one that is not infrequent among political appointments, that in 1783 Sheridan was given the post of Secretary of the Treasury.

As manager of the Drury Lane, Sheridan was at the same time conscientious and unreliable; for instance, although he was backstage every evening to deal with the problems of his company, he rarely sorted through the mail that consequently accumulated by the sackful. As a producer he was impulsive; one of his most notorious errors was to put on *Vortigern*, a play claiming to have been written by Shakespeare but, to the audience on the first night, a palpable forgery.

His two careers made for a hectic life, and the peace of his home during the 1780s was often in danger. The situation was deteriorating, partly on account of his own recklessness, when suddenly real tragedy struck. In 1791 his infant daughter died, and in the following year his wife died of tuberculosis. It was almost twenty years since Richard had rescued her from the clutches of Captain Matthews, and she had left him with many happy memories but also with distinct feelings of guilt over his behaviour during the last few years. He suffered terribly after her death, and so worked harder and drank harder in order to overcome his sufferings. In 1795 he married again, a young woman called Esther Jane Ogle. In the following year, his son Charles was born.

For the next fourteen years or so, Sheridan presented to the public eye the picture of a prosperous man of letters and of government, a great man with a young family and ambitions still waiting to be fulfilled. The Drury Lane was enlarged and reopened, and he achieved a great personal success with his play, *Pizarro*, adapted from a play by August Kotzebue. In 1804 he was appointed Receiver General of the Duchy of Cornwall, and in 1806 became Treasurer of the Navy in the Ministry of All the Talents. In the same year he won the parliamentary seat of Westminster after the death of his old mentor, Charles James Fox.

In 1802, with considerable panache, Sheridan had defeated a bill brought against him in the Court of Chancery by his creditors; this only made them more determined. Drink and debt between them were endangering his health, and to add to his troubles his political life began to decline. After one year as MP for Westminster, he lost his seat there. He was later returned for Ilchester, and finally stood again for Stafford, which had been his very first constituency. He failed to get re-elected; his creditors finally caught up with him, and he was imprisoned for debt; after the three most humiliating days of his life, a few friends supplied the money to bale him out. Between this low point of 1813 and his death at 7 Savile Row on July 7th, 1816, his existence swung between the behaviour appropriate to a grand old man of the theatre, who could utterly charm a dinner table at which sat such guests as Lord Byron, and the squalor of a home oppressed by bailiffs and by disease in both himself and his wife. Maybe he was too proud a man to look for help a second time from the hands that had freed him from prison. When someone did venture into the house, where the couple had grown quite isolated in their misery, it was too late.

After his death, the question was asked as to why nobody had come to his rescue, but it remained unanswered. He was given a splendid funeral and buried in Westminster Abbey; this irony did not go unmarked, at least by the anonymous writer of the following lines:

How proud they can press to the funeral array
Of him whom they shunn'd, in his sickness and sorrow –

How bailiffs may seize his last blanket to-day,
Whose pall shall be held up by Nobles tomorrow!

The wit and good nature that we associate with the young author of *The Rivals* and *The School for Scandal* never entirely left Richard Sheridan. For instance, in February 1809 the enlarged Drury Lane Theatre was destroyed by fire. To us it might seem the low point of his life. Sheridan watched the flames from the Piazza Coffee House and remarked to his friends, 'A man may surely take a glass of wine by his own fireside.' The sad circumstances of his death should not blind us to the varied success of his life. 'Without means, without connexion,' wrote Lord Byron, for whom Sheridan was a legend in his own lifetime, 'he beat them all, in all he ever attempted.'

1.2 BACKGROUND

Consider the progress that Britain was undergoing at the time of the play's writing: it was the era of the Industrial Revolution – of epoch-making inventions in the weaving trade and the mining industry, of Watt's steam engine, of the first iron bridges, of canals and of child labour. It was the era in which the Indian empire became firmly established, the American colonies even more firmly lost. It was an age of travel, and of the grand tour in which a young man was expected to survey the manners and political systems of other nations. It was a time when fortunes were made through commerce and lost through gambling and when a child could be hanged for stealing a handkerchief. Discontent existed beneath the general prosperity, a discontent that was to find expression in the poems of William Blake (1757–1827).

Of all of this there is little or no hint in *The Rivals*. Sheridan depicts an era that was vanishing as he wrote. His world does not belong to professional progress or revolve around the latest scientific discovery; serious discussion about the separation of gases or the implications of electricity is not within the scope of his characters! Their talk is mainly of love, marriage, and of each other. Bernard Shaw, a much more political writer and a socialist, would have made use of technical advances to focus on the corruption of the times; he did so most notably in *The Apple Cart*. But Sheridan the playwright was not primarily interested in political satire or even class satire, dramatic weapons designed to attack the existing social order. He did not seek to demonstrate the possibility of changing the country's economic structure; nor did he wish to blacken the reputation of the court party or the favouritism of King George III. His targets were more domestic but no less universal.

On the other hand, the play is unmistakably Georgian in its tone and attitudes, as well as in the social milieu that it explores. It would be helpful if you would start by jotting down an answer to this broad question: In what ways does our society differ from that represented in *The Rivals*? Think of the domestic arrangements and family relationships, of courtship and education. Keep in mind the class of people with whom the play deals, their tastes and the kinds of entertainment they enjoyed. To fill out your developing portrait of the age you will benefit from looking at some pictures. Sir Joshua Reynolds and Thomas Gainsborough will give you models for the gentry, while Rowlandson and Hogarth will provide you with visual satire of the whole period and of all classes of society.

When one is discussing the social, as opposed to the political, background to a piece of literature, it is often harder to know what to omit than what to include. Sheridan does not allude to many painful aspects of his environment, and maybe it is through a conscious disregard of these aspects that the optimistic mood of the play is achieved. Bath may have been a 'province of pleasure', but its streets, like the streets of London, would have combined the functions of dustbin, sewer and thoroughfare. Sheridan's audience would have been only too well acquainted with the stench, so the author felt no need to refer to it in the dialogue.

Disease was rampant, and that is one reason why Bath was so popular. Typhoid, smallpox, rheumatic fever, gout – all sent their victims rattling down by carriage to this chief spa of England. The infant mortality rate was high and poverty was everywhere, in the towns as in the country. It was not uncommon to find ten people living in an almost unfurnished room; if adults could not eke out a livelihood through casual labour, the workhouse and semi-slavery were the only answer; for once they entered the 'Union' as the workhouse was called, men and women were more or less the property of the factory to which it was attached. Children were made to work in the mines and as sweeps. The age of reform was still half a century away, but as the rumblings of discontent grew louder, riots became increasingly frequent.

The masses hardly exist in the mind of Sir Anthony, and yet his own class is in decline, its power reduced by the simultaneous rise of the commercial magnate and the growth of the vast, aristocratic estate. This decline of the lesser gentry accounts to some extent for the closed world of *The Rivals*. The play itself does not seek to question the social structure, though it recognises many abuses of it; the arranged marriage is a faulty institution, but not without advantages.

Drink and gambling were prevalent vices for all classes; duelling was confined to the upper stratum of society, and crude violence mainly to the lower. Although the policing of the towns was becoming more methodical, it is significant that the Law does not find its way on to King's Mead Fields at the critical moment.

Domestic service employed a huge number of people. Ladies ran the household, they did not run the house. They entertained, often lavishly, and frequently provided musical entertainment themselves, but they did not have to prepare food, bedrooms for guests, or floors for dancing. A lady had to learn to keep accounts, and that is one of Mrs Malaprop's priorities in female education.

Nowadays, men go to the local pub to gossip; in Sheridan's day they would resort to coffee or chocolate houses, like the one in which Sir Lucius has dozed off prior to his first entrance. They were noisy, crowded places, filled with the smoke from clay pipes, but the atmosphere was conducive to business negotiations as well as to scandal or philosophical discussion. Conversation was an art, not simply a means of communication, and a session in the coffee house could last for hours. The park was a centre for intrigue and romantic encounters; there, the ladies indulged their taste for gossip, while keeping an eye out for the latest fashion. It was hard to keep secret anything that happened there, because ladies' maids, like Lucy, seemed to lurk round every corner.

The countryside was becoming more and more like our landscape of today: hedgerows and fields, gardens and fences, with crops in rotation and healthy flocks and herds on plentiful pasture. Enclosure Acts, which allowed farm and common land to be closed off, were frequent and these, together with the manifold improvements brought about by the agricultural revolution, had led to prosperity; unfortunately, as is the wont of such reforms, they also led to massive unemployment, because everywhere manpower was being replaced by machinery; efficiency, as in our own day, was frequently an ally of social distress.

It was the age of landscaped gardens and of the importing of exotic plants and trees. These would have been status symbols, particularly among townsfolk. Mrs Malaprop's drawing-room might be graced by the presence of an enormous fuchsia, that peacock among houseplants.

In spite of the poverty, disease and discontent, it was an age of general well-being and financial stability. The puritan work ethic which regarded the individual's industry as a necessary means of salvation was constructive among the middle stratum of society; Methodism, John Wesley's fervent religion for the poor, who received little solace from the established Church, was an increasingly powerful force among the labouring community, while the rational Christianity of the professional and ruling classes at least allowed for the obligation of Charity, even if it could find no place for a more radical vision. Religion tended to be reduced to a system of morals, and few things were more suspect to the Church of England during this period than emotionalism.

The Georgian age idolised beauty, taste and balance, but at the same time indulged in all kinds of dissipation. In 1773 Horace Walpole, the author, called England 'a gaming, robbing, wrangling, nation without principles, character, or allies; the overgrown shadow of what it was'. Class consciousness was at its strongest, yet freedom was the intellectual's catchword.

Education still tended to concentrate on the classics, but science played an increasingly important part in the curriculum. Women's education was normally of a domestic nature, except where parents discerned a natural talent that needed to be nurtured. It was because so few women engaged in a career that actresses could achieve such a prominent place in society.

Apart from books and newspapers, what were the chief sources for cultural stimulation? The theatre was at the centre of London life. Music was the staple form of family entertainment – young people were expected to play an instrument and to sing; card-playing provided mental excitement as well as an excuse for gambling. Sermons tended to be long, sometimes dreadfully long, and they provided ample matter for discussion round the family table. The clubs, like Brooks's of which Sheridan was a member, provided comfortable surroundings in which men could discuss politics, literature and the state of the world.

In some respects, life was extremely formal. Even when wigs ceased to be worn, the hair was kept long and dressed; women's head-dresses were high and elaborate and their corsets were breathtakingly tight (Lydia has to languish without bending in the middle). Clothes were full, particularly the hooped skirts of the ladies which were so wide that double doors became a necessity as well as a fashion; costume accessories were various and must have been cumbersome: there were canes and snuff-boxes for the men, and perfumed handkerchiefs, smelling salts and, above all, fans for the women. Proper use of the fan required a great deal of practice, because it entailed a language of its own. White gloves and large hats added to ceremony out of doors, and greetings were part of an acquired etiquette. Bows and curtseys could be slight or deep, as occasion demanded, but it would have been rude for a young person to omit some polite gesture when meeting an older person. Hand-kissing was a sign of reverence or affection.

Children were expected to obey their parents in the matters of marriage and career. Because they had no means of earning a living, girls were still very much the property of their fathers; this prompted Sheridan to write to a friend, 'There is not so distressed a situation in the World as that of a Gentleman's Daughter in England left without a Fortune.'

Bath, in Sheridan's youth, was a citadel of pleasure, but according to the accounts of contemporary visitors, it was hardly a citadel that hummed with excitement. 'Mixture of lowliness and grandeur, pride and meanness, politeness and impertinence – Bath – the region of fashion and dullness, of elegance and vapidity, of public reputation and private intrigue, of extravagance and imposition . . . Like a Frenchman's shirt – the ruffle is very fine but the body very coarse.' So wrote Charles Dibdin, actor and writer. The one occupation that employed everyone, it seems, was that of scandal. As the writer Oliver Goldsmith said, 'Scandal must have fixed her throne in Bath preferable to any other part of the Kingdom.' This is not to discredit the intention of those many invalids who went to Bath to take the waters, hoping for a cure. They were attended in their suffering by every kind of inconvenience, from rain and the commotion of society to 'the flavour of the waters themselves, which many found unpalatable. As a city, Bath prospered, and for this it had to thank both invalids, and visitors in search of pleasure.

2 THE THEATRE

2.1 THE BUILDING

In the early years of the eighteenth century, there was a proliferation of what we would call 'fringe theatres' but there were only three playhouses in Georgian London patented to present plays on a professional basis. Covent Garden and the Drury Lane had received their patents when Charles II was restored to the throne in 1660 and the Theatrical Licensing Act, introduced by Walpole in 1737 to prevent political satire, which was at the time largely aimed at himself, firmly confined play-acting to these two great theatres. The third theatre, the Haymarket, only enjoyed its full patent from 1766-77, and thereafter presented summer seasons.

Covent Garden housed the first production of *The Rivals*, while the Drury Lane theatre was to become home from home to Sheridan after he became its manager.

Since none of these buildings exists in anything like its true eighteenth-century shape, you will have to visit the Bristol Old Vic (The Theatre Royal, built 1766) for a living example of the kind of theatre in which Sheridan's plays were originally acted. It is a good example, for the designs show that it was a replica in many ways of its London predecessors.

The buildings were small, the space remarkably intimate; the audiences were often disproportionately large, for there was no numbered seating and no maximum number to be admitted, as there is nowadays in any theatre that hopes to survive. Covent Garden could hold around 1300 and Drury Lane 1200. The auditorium was divided into pit (our stalls), boxes, first gallery and second gallery ('the gods'). The decoration was ornate, even sumptuous. The seating was not; it consisted mainly of benches.

There was only one entrance to the pit, and access to the other levels was along narrow, poorly lit passages, where pickpockets found ample opportunity for their talents.

Between the pit and the stage lay the sunken orchestra pit; then came the forestage or 'apron' as we call it, with the footlights running along its edge. The proscenium arch divided the forestage from the main acting area. The curtains hung behind the proscenium; during a performance, they were draped up and away from the stage, but were left visible in order to give definition to the stage picture. Another feature of the stage that no longer exists except where imitation is intended, was the doors that stood on either side of the forestage and which were used for many exits and entrances. These doors had a hundred years of history behind them. Upstage (to use theatrical vocabulary) beyond the main acting area, the scenery was displayed, so the stage had considerable depth to it. Its width was thirty-six feet, and on either side there were ten feet of wing space. The auditorium was cramped by comparison.

The Rivals was not originally performed to a group of benevolent spectators in a darkened auditorium, who had come to watch a classic before or after dinner. The mood was not one of respectful pleasure but of critical delight and keen participation. Some audience members in the pit and boxes were almost close enough to touch Faulkland or Jack when one of them delivered an aside. The atmosphere, considering the compact nature of the auditorium and the fact that it was well lit by candles, must have united actors and spectators in a bond of mutual laughter. People were expected to voice and clap their approval of Julia and to comment openly on the ridiculous behaviour of others. Sheridan and Goldsmith made of the Georgian theatre a place where social folly was once more a communal concern.

Taken as a whole, backstage was much larger than front of house. Corridors ran round the walls enclosing the stage area, allowing actors to move easily from one side to the other; dressing rooms were located off these corridors; although there were a good number of these, there must have been some crowding; in the 1777–8 season at Drury Lane there were forty-five actors, twenty-seven actresses, fourteen dancers and five singers. The dressing-rooms were not uncomfortable, however, and most of them had stoves. In the flies above the stage, and underneath it, was elaborate machinery, which was particularly used in pantomime. There were traps and bridges and drums and pulleys for creating all sorts of transformation effects and sudden appearances. The enormous cellar contained a rehearsal room for dancers, the musicians' sitting-room, a music library, and storage space for lights and props.

The whole building was practical in its design, and was intended to provide the management with a commercial proposition for the presenting of plays. The public paid for entertainment, not for comfort.

2.2 THE AUDIENCE

The cost of a seat was one shilling in the second gallery, two shillings in the first gallery, three in the pit, and five in a box. If the house was kept full, a handsome profit could be made. A shilling in those days would have bought a 4lb loaf.

It has been assessed that the theatre-going public during Sheridan's heyday was approximately 12 000. Allowing for the fact that its more eager members would gladly see a play more than once, and that some frequented the theatre three or four times a week, no matter what was showing, this potential audience number still did not allow the management the leisure of offering a month's run, or even a week's. Far from it: it was customary to present a different play on each of the six days in the week.

To see a play, the audience sometimes had to queue outside the theatre for hours, because there was no advance booking, except for the boxes. It was cold waiting outside the theatre, and not much warmer inside it; there was no heating in the auditorium. Once seated, there would be another long wait for those who had arrived early enough to ensure a good place for themselves. One had to while away an hour munching fruit purchased from the orange-seller, and in chatting to one's neighbour; but it was noisy, uncomfortable and often smelly, so friends would take it in turns to guard their seats, while the rest went out for a stroll or a glass of ale. Covent Garden teemed with pickpockets, prostitutes and young show-offs, who were commonly known as 'bucks'. All life may have been there, but who would have endured it for the sake of a play?

First of all, let us be clear about what they were getting for their money. In our affluent but hurried days, it is not uncommon for play-goers to be charged a fairly large sum of money to see a show that will last around two and a half hours. They expect to see one play with probably one interval, four or five actors and one set. The Georgian audience required and expected considerably more: an entertainment lasting between three and a half and five hours, consisting of a play and an after-play, and supplemented by short entr'actes of singing and dancing. An evening at the theatre meant what it said. *The Rivals* was originally accompanied by its quota of entr'actes and an after-play entitled *The Druids*, which was performed 'By Particular Desire'. The management was clearly intent on providing something for everyone.

The play started at 6.00 or 6.15 pm. The area surrounding the theatres became increasingly disreputable during Sheridan's day, so that the late hour at which the curtain fell, the dim lighting in the streets, and the dangers lurking there used to deter some of the wealthier and more aristo-cratic patrons from attendance. Nevertheless, the theatres maintained their rank as halls of fashion as well as of culture.

The boxes were reserved, often by subscription or season ticket, for the cream of society, titled folk, and the Royal Family. There is in existence a lady's fan that shows on the slats the whole circle of boxes and the name of the subscriber for each one: a very nice aid to spying. The boxes were at the first level: an actor could reach out and touch the closest ones on either side of the stage. They were well lit throughout the performance and visible from most parts of the house; this enabled the great and wealthy to be seen, to watch each other, to examine who was accompanying whom, to parade their finery; in short, to be part of the performance.

In the pit sat the professional people – lawyers, doctors, writers, and, of course, the critics. The serious business of watching and dissecting a play went on here, and disapproval from the pit could prove almost as much of an embarrassment as an F on an exam paper. Critics were often factious, but they were not easy to ignore and unless bribery and corruption rendered them suspect, they were the allowed arbiters of taste and good sense, though there were always amateurs ready to challenge their authority.

Above the boxes was the first gallery, where tradesmen, shopkeepers and businessmen sat with their families. It was a fairly orderly place, inhabited by good citizens who wanted entertainment without much fuss. They knew what they wanted, and were slow to appreciate changes in style and presentation.

The second gallery was traditionally the home of domestic servants, labourers and sailors on leave, and also of the rowdies. If 'the gods' disapproved, the actors and the audience knew it. Insults, orange peel and sometimes vegetables were flung at the stage; it was not unknown for a glass, a bottle or 'a pound of brass' to cause an accident among the audience, and on at least one occasion a man was thrown out of the second gallery. Several riots are recorded; the most famous one started when the theatre took away the privilege of paying only half-price to enter after the third act. That custom was soon reinstated.

There was another, final group, and they too could be troublesome. These were 'the bucks', young beaux and fops who liked to sit on the edge of the stage during a performance: from there they could throw witticisms at the actors, provoke the audience and generally make a nuisance of themselves. It was Sheridan himself who eventually managed to dislodge them, though not before most of his plays had suffered from their rudeness.

The Georgian period was one in which social mobility was considered of less importance than the acceptance of one's proper position in society. The public seem not to have questioned to which level of the auditorium they belonged, though if a seaman or servant could pay more, he could presumably go down lower.

One practice that caused a lot of argument was that of servants keeping their masters' places in the boxes. They were allowed to reserve the seat by sitting on it, but this would sometimes cause consternation, when a well-bred group, longing perhaps to engage in scandal, found its conversation impeded by the silent presence of a footman. For the sake of convenience, however, the custom prevailed.

2.3 THE PLAYS

In the arts, particularly in literature, this was the age of sensibility, of refined and delicate emotional responses. There was 'a decorum in these matters', and offence against that decorum was likely to provoke derision.

It used to be assumed that what we call sentimental comedy was the dominant genre in eighteenth-century drama. Although more recent research has made it clear that this is an exaggeration in numerical terms, and that only one-sixth of the plays fall into that category, there is no reason to suggest that it was not the most influential form in matters of style, theme and impact.

The reforming of a libertine; the heroic sacrifice of a loving wife; maidenly distress; the correct matching of fortune with fortune; the punishment of vice and the reward of virtue; examples of honesty allied to good breeding – these were the stuff of the drama when Sheridan appeared. They add up to an art based on the twin notions of poetic justice and gentle manners.

Certain ways in which Shakespeare's plays were adapted give us a good idea of what the age thought unacceptable, and of the extreme sensibility that it applauded. Do you know the tomb scene in *Romeo and Juliet*? Romeo returns from Mantua, having been told that his wife has died and been buried in the family vault. When he finds Juliet, whose death is in fact only a disguise induced by a drug, he takes his leave of her with a kiss, drinks a poison and dies. When Juliet wakes to find Romeo dead beside her, she kills herself with his dagger rather than leave the tomb with Friar Lawrence, who is urging her to go with him. Although this suited Shakespeare, it did not suit Garrick or his audience. This is how Garrick's version goes:

(When Juliet wakes, Romeo is still alive; just.)

JULIET   And did I wake for this?

ROMEO   My powers are blasted, 'Twixt death and love I am torn –
I am distracted! But death's strongest – and must I leave
thee, Juliet?
O cruel, cursed fate: in spite of heav'n!

JULIET   Thou rav'st – lean on my breast –

ROMEO   Fathers have flinty hearts, no tears can melt 'em. Nature
pleads in vain – Children must be wretched.

JULIET   O my breaking heart –

ROMEO   She is my wife – our hearts are twined together, Capulet
forbear – Paris, loose your hold – Pull not our heart
strings thus – they crack – they break –
Oh Juliet, Juliet!

(Dies)

Most of us would say that is milking it; to the eighteenth century it meant passion and tears. The *London Chronicle* voiced the general approval: 'Had Shakespeare seen the original, he would never have omitted such a fine dramatic incident.' Do you sense the same yearning love mood in the following lines?

> ...and while the freezing blast numbed our joints, how warmly would he press me to pity his flame, and glow with mutual ardour
> (*The Rivals*, V.i)

It was an age of revivals, and it was hard to get a new play produced. Sheridan was one major dramatist, and Goldsmith was the other. He wrote *She Stoops to Conquer* some two years before *The Rivals* was put on, and Sheridan owes a certain amount to the earlier play, in particular to its tone. Goldsmith wrote in his 'Comparison of Laughing and Sentimental Comedy' that the sentimental variety was a 'species of Bastard Tragedy' and that in it 'the Virtues of Private Life are exhibited, rather than the Vices exposed'. Both he and Sheridan were resolved to tackle the domestic vices, though in such a manner as to raise the laughter of understanding rather than a storm of disgust. They forged a new direction for eighteenth-century comedy by returning more wholeheartedly than their contemporaries to the Comedy of Manners.

2.4 THE COMEDY OF MANNERS

This theatrical genre is distinguished from other types of comedy, i.e. situation comedy, romantic comedy, slapstick, farce, mainly by the aims of the playwright. The main sources for the laughter he provokes are not situation and sexual intrigue, nor even character, though all these have their contribution to make; his focus is on the foibles of high society, his targets are the follies of fashion and social pretension; to a greater or lesser extent there is an inherent desire to reform the ills that are exposed. Any attempt at reform relies on humour rather than on a dramatic sermon. The weapons at the author's disposal are wit and the lack of it (as with Captain Absolute and Bob Acres); the gulling or making a fool of someone (i.e. Mrs Malaprop); comic obsession (Faulkland) and ignorance of self (Lydia); the aping of good manners by a character who lacks them (Acres); and character as an expression of commonly held but suspect ideas (Sir Anthony). All the items at which the Comedy of Manners pokes fun are in the first instance highly characteristic of the period in which it is written, but they become universal because human nature does not change that much, though its clothing does.

When Sheridan took up the pen, it was as a pupil, not of his immediate predecessors, but of William Congreve, the great master of high comedy during the late Restoration period, (1670–1729). In a Comedy of Manners there is always an element of social satire. In *Volpone* by Ben Jonson, *Tartuffe* by Molière, the *Way of the World* by Congreve and, to a lesser extent, *The School for Scandal* by Sheridan, it has a strong and bitter flavour; here we meet extremes of vice, hypocrisy and greed. In *Love for Love* by Congreve, and *The Rivals*, the satire is gentler; the society it depicts is less brittle, or less brutal. Of all the plays of its kind, *The Rivals* must be about the most robust, a word that Sheridan himself used to describe it.

2.5 THE ACTORS

There was no director as such, no one to unify a production. While this may have permitted actors to work together in a fruitful manner, it gave rise to a virtuosity that could be disruptive. Can you imagine a two-week rehearsal period, with each actor deciding for himself where the focus should be at any given moment? There was little guidance from out front, because the actor-manager was usually in the play. He sometimes instructed 'such young or other performers, as might be likely to derive advantage from a knowledge acquired by many years' observation and considerable practice'. This did not amount to training and must have consisted largely of tips about physical and vocal technique.

Finding your way about the stage was mostly a question of being in the right place for the delivery of your next line. No wonder that one foreign visitor said that English actors always seemed to be looking for each other. Take a look at the last scene of *The Rivals* with this traffic problem in mind: it must have looked like Hyde Park on a sunny afternoon.

What about the acting itself? David Garrick set the pace for the age, and he was known best of all for his sudden, psychological turns, and for his realistic portrayal of emotions, particularly of conflicting ones; his face, his hands, his very nerves were made to express mood and intention. He taught the audience 'those nice touches of nature which they were till then strangers to. When he acted, the audience saw what was right' – so wrote a critic, looking back over the golden age of Garrick. The style of acting that he developed was particularly successful in comedy, and would have been employed by Mr Woodward, Mrs Bulkley and the rest in the first production of *The Rivals*. One of the company, Mr Shuter, who played Sir Anthony, was occasionally guilty of overacting, and the *Theatrical Examiner* took him to task for this: 'Be comic, Mr. S-r! not too comical! you can make your face mighty droll: but twisting wry faces is not always just and humorous.'

The audience expected to see the details of nature in action and reaction. This does not mean that they or the actors had any concept of a 'fourth wall' that exists invisibly between the stage and auditorium. On the contrary, the convention was very much that of 'out-front delivery' - of facing the audience rather than one's partner. The face and the eyes were given particular importance, and the shadowing bulk of wig, headdress or hat demanded that the actor 'cheat out', or face the audience, much of the time.

It was extremely hard work being a member of either company. To retain three or four, sometimes many more, roles in one's mind, is an exacting business. Fortunately, receiving a prompt was easier under the comparatively dim lighting.

As for the actor's social status, a German traveller, F. A. Wendeborn wrote in his book, *A View of England*:

> I need not mention that the character of a player has nothing degrading in England, and that those who are at the head of the profession are rather courted, even by people of rank, and introduced into the best companies. In France they have hitherto denied an actor, or an actress, what is called a Christian burial; in England, players are interred with magnificence in Westminster Abbey.

One of the actor's duties was to be the arbiter of pronunciation; it was largely owing to the 'drayma' (as 'drama' was pronounced) that the concept of standard English developed.

2.6 COSTUME

The attitude to costume in this era was simultaneously practical and, we should say, primitive. It was practical in so far as it did not thrust on the audience a historical authenticity for which they had neither the eye nor the interest. It was primitive for the same reason: it allowed a wide divergence of styles during the same production. This was sometimes true of the costumes in a contemporary play like *The Rivals*, because on the whole it was a matter of fancy: leading actors were permitted to find their own costumes, independent of each other. It was a colourful period for clothes, so there must have been some barbarous clashes.

As an example of what could happen in the historical drama, take one actor who was playing a Roman hero. He turned up with his favourite costume in the latest fashion: powdered wig, boots, lace, breeches with buckles, and plumed hat; to greet him the assembled company were dressed in wildly inauthentic Roman garb. To us it smacks of Frankie Howerd, but they took one look and got on with the job.

There was still a tradition, as in Shakespeare's day, for wealthy and aristocratic personages to hand down their cast-off clothes to actors. Some of them were splendid, some were undeniably threadbare, and as lighting improved, the difference became more obvious. Extravagance in costume was, as always, part of the fun. Some of the trimming, for instance, was made of real gold and silver.

Each company built up a wardrobe of 'types', particularly for small parts. There would also be sets of costumes, or at least of accessories, for different periods, but the thirst for historical realism was confined to the actor's study. Garrick as Hamlet or King Lear looked like a contemporary of the Absolutes, though there was admittedly some critical distaste at his anachronistic use of a handkerchief to dry his eyes when he played King Lear.

From the point of view of your trying to visualise *The Rivals*, nothing is more important than a sense of costume. These people do not wear jeans and sweat shirts. The ladies' dresses in 1775 were a very peculiar shape, so wide and somehow like travelling tables! It may seem preferable to set the play some ten years later when the silhouettes are softer and more romantic, though this does make Mrs Malaprop a less ridiculous being to observe as she trundles around the stage trying to look delicate. Look around you. What are the ridiculous fashions of today? Sheridan did not really have to think about how to costume his play, at least not in the way we do.

2.7 SCENERY

Scenic designs were painted on upright flats (known earlier in the century as 'shutters') and there were five sets of these on either side of the stage. These sets, consisting of representations of interiors, parades and so on, were fixed at intervals of six feet, and all ran parallel to the edge of the stage. The painting on them made some concession to perspective, but this could not help but be distorted by the proximity of an actor.

Cut into the raked (upwardly sloping away from the audience) floor of the stage, were sets of grooves with raised edges. The flats slid along these grooves when being moved on or off stage for a new scene. The grooves themselves could be removed, and had to be for ballet. Actors were amazingly adept at avoiding these little obstacles, and although one or two in the full flood of passion had been known to trip, this was a rare occurrence.

Beyond the flats, heading off-stage on either side of it, were 'wings', which were not necessarily consistent in design with the flats themselves. Behind these wings, the flats that had just been used or which were about to be drawn on stage, were stored. At the back of the stage the flats met in the middle, so as to create a rear wall or a deepening perspective; and at the end of each act, a painted cloth fell just behind the curtain line.

The scene changes were rapid, and no attempt was made to conceal them. Very often the actors did not leave the stage, but the scenery did. Again, these changing 'views', which could be as many as twenty-five for a spectacular show like a pantomime, were an integral part of what the audience paid for and expected. Fifteen men or more might be employed to change the scenery, and they cannot have been as quiet as mice.

Each theatre had its collection of stock sets of 'views': temples, tombs, city walls and gates, palaces, streets, a chamber, a prison, gardens, and groves. By clever permutation these could cover any contingency, including some that were never intended by the designer. The following quotation is taken from a review in the *True Briton*, of a production of Shakespeare's *The Merchant of Venice*:

> On Saturday an obtrusive Grove came between the partition of a Room and plenty of trees gave evidence in the Hall of Justice.

Such errors were more frequent, and more readily forgiven by audiences, than in today's professional theatre; but the eighteenth century enjoyed a sense of childlike wonder at the pomp of show and the passing of life upon the stage.

Our theatre is much more technically orientated, but it is necessary for the designer of *The Rivals* to take into account the facilities, as well as the 'sense of wonder', that would have existed at the time when it was first staged.

For instance, one can see how Sheridan has arranged for the Parades to cover the drawing out of other 'views'; and one can estimate that he envisaged the use of eight different scenes of contrasting kinds. It is evident that he could rely on a scene change to shift location quickly: he takes us from Mrs Malaprop's lodgings to those of Capt. Absolute, so the interiors must have been very different and readily identifiable.

We know from the original poster that the first production was endowed with 'NEW SCENES', so the painting would have been fresh and the element of spectacle greater than we might associate with the play when we are simply reading it.

As so often, the question is, what use can the designer make of his or her knowledge of the period? Most theatres are not equipped with the resources to reconstruct grooves and sliding flats, even if that were desirable. In our day, we tend to require a greater realism of the individual set, or alternatively audiences like to be surprised by technological brilliance. There are ways, though, of recapturing the business and the sense of magic which formed a part of eighteenth-century staging and design. One way is to have a single set, which is flexible: pieces can be 'trucked' in and out, or rotated, to present different rooms or exteriors. Backdrops can be used to good effect, while motifs for particular settings can be 'flown in'. Another aspect of the play's background that a designer might wish to explore is that of the original stage machinery: pulleys and winches, and even a minimal use of sliding flats, candelabra and perspective scenery. All these things have to be filtered through the imagination, so that the design is modern and authentic to our age, not just historically correct.

The furniture, similarly, can comment on the scene in hand. Mrs Malaprop would probably not have the same kind of chairs as Capt. Absolute. On the other hand, a designer might decide to keep the same furniture throughout, and just to adorn it with different upholstery or cushions when the scene is changed. Perhaps the furniture itself is made, if there is enough money for such an extravagance, in a style that slightly caricatures that of the original period. The eighteenth-century theatre used furniture sparsely, and any director of the play needs to consider very carefully how he is going to assemble chairs, tables and settees for each new scene, before deciding to reproduce exactly the picturesque interiors of Bath. Either a great deal of money, or a great deal of simplifying, is required before the play becomes visually manageable.

The physical nature of the Parades presents a problem for the designer. They have to be changed quickly, and should create an immediate atmosphere; to preserve the idea of a street and of the interlude quality of the scenes that take place on it, they should not use the whole depth of the stage. The most ingenious solution I have seen was in the form of a pair of folding screens which could be pulled out from either side of the stage; on each was painted a row of houses, the tops of which were cut out to form a silhouette; one contained an arch through which actors could stoop slightly to make entrances and exits; at no point were the screens much taller than the actors, so that the effect was of architecture in miniature.

All of this adds up to one question. When each scene begins, what do you see in front of you? If it is no more than lines on the printed page, stir your imagination!

2.8 LIGHTING

This was an age of innovation in stage lighting. The first important step, in 1765, was taken by Garrick, who removed the massive chandeliers that had hung over the middle of every London stage since the theatres re-opened after the Commonwealth. Instead, lights were suspended behind the proscenium arch on vertical strips of metal; each light had a reflector and a shield, which could be used to increase or diminish brightness, as needed.

The footlights along the edge of the forestage were a crude but effective device: a long row of pairs of candles on saucer-like bases, floating on oil which acted as fuel for them. The whole burning flotilla was contained in the 'footlight trap' which could be completely lowered out of sight by pulleys, when darkness was required. Other sources of illumination were the auditorium lights which could not be extinguished during a performance, and oil lamps and candles concealed behind the 'wings'. The cost of candles for one season was about £800 for the entire theatre.

During this period, Phillip James de Loutherbourg was in the process of revolutionising the art of lighting. He was able to create beautiful effects with light and shade by using reflectors and dimming devices; he developed the technique of transparencies – special silk screens for effects like clouds and sunsets – and another technique of placing gauze in front of a light to produce the impression that the performers were 'aerial beings'. With all that fire on or near the stage, it was a hot place to be, and it was not uncommon for an audience to be aware of a gently rising haze that surrounded the actors.

Lighting must have contributed strongly to the varied atmosphere of *The Rivals*, when it was first produced. Julia and Lydia together must have been something of a fragile dream, while Mrs Malaprop could have used the natural shadows to conceal her as she spied on her niece and Capt. Absolute. And imagine Faulkland, right downstage, with his face made lurid by the flickering footlights, as he upbraids himself for his final unkindness to Julia, ' – O fool! – dolt! – barbarian!' Yes, it was probably funny, but disturbing at the same time. Candlelight can obviously assist a love scene, but its inconsistency can be made to contribute to any kind of emotional scene; no doubt Mr Shuter as Sir Anthony found a way to use the light to his advantage when twisting his 'wry faces'.

We can do many remarkable things with lights nowadays, yet it is hard to recreate the feeling of an illuminated theatre before even gaslight was invented. The tendency is to create atmospheric lighting for each of the scenes and to support the changes with appropriate harpsichord music, or bird-song for the open air effects of the last scene! While elaborate lighting can help to embody the world of the play and to make for a fluent production, this very fluency and filmlike realism can sometimes destroy the audience's intimate relationship to the stage. A compromise needs to be made between the old and the new.

2.9 STAGE HISTORY OF THE PLAY

The play has never quite been able to compete for popularity with *The School for Scandal*. In tone the difference between the two resembles that between Bath and London. The later play has a greater range of characters, and more bite in the satire. There is an element of real vice and hypocrisy in Joseph Surface, Lady Sneerwell and Snake which we shall not find in the earlier play. The wit is urbane in *The School for Scandal*, and Mrs Candour and her circle make a profession of gossip and slander in a way that far outdoes Mrs Malaprop's provincial follies. The danger into which Lady Teazle runs and the comic tension in the famous screen scene, as well as its dramatic and emotional outcome, lend a depth to the play that is absent from *The Rivals*.

Sheridan was rarely observed at work, and when *The School for Scandal* was first produced in 1777, it was found to be so different from *The Rivals* that many members of the London theatre-going public believed it was not his work. There was even a rumour that it had been written by a young lady, the daughter of a merchant, who had submitted the manuscript to Sheridan as manager of the Drury Lane and had then expired. The controversy over authorship did not detract from the play's overwhelming success; on its first night, it was greeted with such thunderous applause that a passer-by fled for his life thinking the theatre was about to collapse. No comedy of manners has so constantly met with the public's favour.

The Rivals cannot claim such an august history, but it too has enjoyed two centuries' worth of revivals. Sheridan earned only £600 from the original, but even that was £100 more than Goldsmith earned for *She Stoops to Conquer*. Within months of its opening it could be seen at Bath, where it has remained a favourite for obvious reasons. Throughout the nineteenth century it was revived by touring companies and in London. As realism became more and more dominant, the production style of period plays tended to surrender to its demands. Although 1840-70 seem to have been the years when *The Rivals* was most constantly revived, the grandest productions came towards the end of the century. In 1884 the Bancrofts staged the play as a full-blown exhibition of the eighteenth-century milieu. Research was carried out at the British Museum; architecture, furniture and costumes of the period were strictly scrutinised and reproduced. One can imagine that the result was a little too worthy, if authentic.

In the annals for Stratford-upon-Avon, from the latter part of the nineteenth century until 1927, Sheridan appears as the most revived playwright apart from Shakespeare. During those years *The Rivals* was produced, on average, every five years, only once less than *The School for Scandal*.

During this century the play has rarely been off the boards. It has had big, West End revivals, and innumerable repertory company productions. The spectacular production by Peter Wood at the National Theatre in 1983 had much about it that was excellent. The play rolled along with a mixture of refinement and gusto and only seemed to flag when actors did not relish the language and the action sufficiently. Michael Hordern as Sir Anthony and Geraldine McEwan as Mrs Malaprop were very fine; they lived the style, they did not put it on like fancy dress. The Olivier stage was a far cry from that of Covent Garden in 1775. The designer John Gunter was highly inventive in the way in which he filled in the vast open space and made it adapt to the more intimate requirements of the interiors.

David Garrick, manager of Covent Garden's rival theatre, the Drury Lane, attended the second performance of *The Rivals*, after Sheridan had spent eleven days ridding the script of the faults for which the first night audience had condemned it. Early in the evening the great man of the theatre remarked, 'I see this play will creep.' At the end of the evening he was forced to say, 'I see this play will run.' It has been running ever since.

The drama critic, W. A. Darlington wrote that 'Sheridan the dramatist is alive to-day and has never consented to moulder on the shelves along with the other "classics". He is more vibrantly alive than any other of the old dramatists excepting only Shakespeare.'

3 SUMMARY AND CRITICAL COMMENTARY

The preface

The author begins by saying that normally he would dispense with a preface, a convention which he compares to a plea of innocence after a guilty verdict. The unprecedented circumstance that prompted him to compose one was the withdrawal of the play after the first night, in order that its obvious flaws might be corrected. So the preface is in part an apology, and in part a justification; it is delicately phrased, and allows him to sketch a fairly convincing self-portrait of Richard Sheridan as a literary innocent. But it is hard to tell how far the playwright is speaking in character. When he says that he was happily ignorant of plays in general, and was thereby freed from the dangers of plagiarism and from having a mind full of precedents, is he not speaking relatively? Could the son of Thomas Sheridan have escaped his theatrical upbringing with so light a burden of knowledge?

For the errors in the original script, including its inordinate length, he blames himself; they proceeded, he says, from inexperience. Mr Harris, the manager of the Theatre Royal in Covent Garden, had considerably curtailed the play, but not enough: he had not wished to hurt the feelings of his young protégé, and his only mistake had been that of indulgence towards the 'vanity of a young author'.

His greatest error, he confesses, lay in his treatment of Sir Lucius, though once again he protests that any malice perceived had been entirely unintended; most of the textual changes after the first night had been to do with Sir Lucius; in the first script he was altogether more brutal than in the printed edition. He was the stage Irishman taken to extremes, and was offensive to many at a time when the Irish question was sensitive. The character had also been played too coarsely for the audience's taste, so the actor was replaced for the second and subsequent performances. Sheridan seizes the opportunity of the preface to disclaim any intention of adverse 'national reflection' in the portrait. On the contrary, he says, he would have rejoiced to see the play fail, if only its condemnation could have added 'one spark to the decaying flame of national attachment' to Ireland. There is probably only the slightest touch of blarney about this, because all through his public life Richard Sheridan was to remain dedicated to the cause of justice in his country of origin.

On one score our author is positively blunt. While he regards the first-night audience as a reliable guide, even if rude, he has no time for 'puny little critics' who condemn out of malice or jealousy.

The preface ends with a heartfelt vote of thanks to the company at Covent Garden, and by recommending that theatre to aspiring playwrights.

The first prologue

The first prologue, between the Serjeant-at-Law (or Barrister) and the Attorney (Solicitor) is a method of disarming the audience's judgement. Sheridan simply tells the audience how kind they are looking; he can't imagine such a jury frowning, hissing or groaning. Of such a well-wishing crowd what author could be afraid? So let *The Rivals* begin, and who can doubt its success? That is the general effect of this dialogue, and the Serjeant's speech on behalf of the poet bears the stamp of his client's confidence, though his earlier lines:

> Yet tell your client, that, in adverse days,
> This wig is warmer than a bush of bays.

struck a warning note. Sheridan, after all, had abandoned his legal wig in favour of the poet's laurel, and he faced the cold if *The Rivals* should fail.

The second prologue

This is a more conventional piece of writing than its predecessor. The Restoration prologue was usually a single verse speech of this kind and was spoken by a leading actor or actress in order to dispose the audience favourably to the evening's entertainment. In tune with the age for which he wrote, Sheridan's prologue is less flirtatious and more edifying. Since it was composed to be spoken on the tenth night by Mrs Bulkley, who played Julia, it no longer needed to be a plea for approval, for that had already been given; the play had enjoyed a long run for those days.

What the author gives us here is a piece of dramatic criticism, which assumes agreement from the discerning, in favour of 'laughing comedy' as opposed to 'preaching comedy'. The author can afford to ride his hobby-horse in public when it has already stayed the course. Comedy that is not didactic, that is what he favours. The actress points to the statue of Comedy on one side of the stage:

Look on her well - does she seem formed to teach?
Should you expect to see this lady - preach?

Then she points to the statue of Tragedy, and argues against the sentimental Muse who would infuse tragic themes into light matter.

Both prologues help to remind us that Sheridan had long practised the
craft of a poet; his couplets are witty and pleasing to the ear, and his
rhymes are, for the most part, unforced.

Before the action begins

The play begins at the point where various strands of action are about to
converge. Some things have already happened about which we need to be
quite clear if we are to understand the development of the plot.

Lydia Languish and Captain Absolute have fallen in love. To satisfy
her romantic ideals, he has adopted the alias of a poor soldier, one Ensign
Beverley; she does not in the least suspect his true identity. Lydia lives
with her widowed Aunt, Mrs Malaprop, who has 'interceded' their correspondence, and in outrage at its contents has shut Lydia up in her room.
She is particularly upset by the very fact that so pleases her niece: that
this Ensign Beverley has not a penny to his name, while Lydia is an heiress.
Mrs Malaprop and Sir Anthony have reached the beginnings of an understanding with regard to a match between her niece and his son, little
thinking how far this has already developed.

Bob Acres' prior suit to Lydia has already been relegated to a lower
shelf in Mrs Malaprop's mind, because she considers him socially inferior.
Bob for his part does not seem particularly set on Lydia for herself, but
he thinks she is beautiful and knows she is rich, and has somehow convinced himself that he's in with a chance; it was his mother who engineered
the match and who sent him to Bath to pursue it, and to pick up a little
urban *savoir-faire* into the bargain. He has seen Julia lately in Devon,
because he lives only a mile from Sir Anthony Absolute, her guardian.

Julia and Faulkand fell in love, and when he saved her from drowning,
this seemed to put a seal on the match, in spite of Lydia's caustic comment
that 'a water-spaniel would have done as much'. Unfortunately for everyone
concerned, but particularly for Julia, Faulkland is such a ditherer that he
keeps postponing the happy event.

It is Sir Anthony's gout that propels him to Bath. There he surprises
Fag, his son's servant, in the street, and, to avoid having to betray his
master, Fag says the Captain has come to Bath to recruit soldiers.

Sir Lucius has been writing love-letters to Mrs Malaprop, under the
misapprehension that he was addressing himself to Lydia. He has been
misled by the mercenary Lucy, Lydia's maid, who is scheming indis-

criminately for all parties as long as they pay up, and consequently knows more about what is going on than anyone else on the stage; but even she does not know the true identity of Ensign Beverley.

All this exposition is cunningly introduced into the dialogue of the first three scenes of the play. Sheridan is in no hurry to get it over with, partly because it is important to the whole structure, but partly because it occasions much incidental laughter, which is always helpful to a comedy in its early stages. We are fortunate that this play is written tightly enough to require only these few paragraphs of introduction. Many comedies of manners, such as Congreve's *The Way of the World*, would require a great deal more labour to reveal their foundations.

Act I, Scene i

Summary
Fag, Captain Absolute's servant, and Thomas, Sir Anthony's coachman, meet by chance in the street. By means of their conversation, most of the major facets of the story are introduced: Captain Absolute's adopted name and the reason for it; Lydia's fortune and her romantic yearning for poverty; the existence of a tough old aunt; Sir Anthony's gout and bad temper; the prospective marriage between Julia and Faulkland; and the social climate of Bath.

Commentary
'Enter Thomas; he crosses the stage; Fag follows, looking after him.' During this scene, as with the prologues, the audience remains aware of the stage as a stage, a platform from which introductions are made, where the basic ingredients of the plot are mentioned, and the society and habits of Bath depicted with a few bold strokes. There is little padding around the exposition, but Fag and Thomas are given sufficient character to awaken our interest in them.

Thomas the coachman does not appear again, but Sheridan, always a careful writer and reviser of his work, has taken pains over the old retainer, who, like mariners in Victorian melodrama, speaks in metaphors drawn from his function – 'I wish they were harnessed together in matrimony'. His refusal to discard his wig, and his local references to Jack Gauge the exciseman and Dick the farrier give his character flesh and blood and lend him some existence apart from the mere imparting of information. The taunts of his fellow servant permit the author to touch on the differences between old and young, and between simplicity and pretension, which will become major themes in the play. We find there is snobbery downstairs, just as there is upstairs.

Fag, who is to play such a large part in the comic intrigue, requires more careful attention from the audience, so the author has given a good many hints as to his character, bearing and voice. He apes his master, but goes beyond Captain Absolute in his desire to be a man of fashion. London is his proper domain, not Bath, where his spirit is kept in check by the 'regular hours'. He is a self-appointed leader in the beau monde of upper-class service; manners and money are his major concerns. We enjoy laughing at him, but as with all the characters in this play, the laughter is gentle and no serious satire is intended. Although we laugh *at* his pretensions: 'none of the London whips of any degree of ton wear wigs now', we laugh *with* him in his quick-wittedness. Like the actor playing the part, you need to have a clear idea of why he reacts to Thomas's news as he does. The exposition in the scene is abundant. What does Sheridan most need to get across? Capt. Absolute's disguise? The arrival of Sir Anthony and Julia?

The only characters of whose existence we are ignorant by the end of this short scene are Acres and David, and Sir Lucius O'Trigger; they form a different strand of the plot, and Sheridan needs to reserve them, like comic cards or jokers, up his sleeve.

Perhaps the most resonant line in the scene is Fag's; 'Why then, the cause of all this is – Love, – Love, Thomas . . . . '. This prepares us for the main preoccupation of the play.

Act I, Scene ii

Summary

Lucy supplies her mistress with volumes of fiction from the circulating libraries of Bath. Julia's unexpected arrival is the cue for a tale of woe from Lydia; she gives an account of recent events to do with her 'connection with Beverley', announces sensationally that she has 'lost him', and explains how Mrs Malaprop's revenge is the cause of her present confinement, her aunt having intercepted an incriminating note from Beverley.

With Lydia, one subject runs automatically into another, and she introduces with great glee the notion that Mrs Malaprop has found herself a suitor, a 'tall Irish baronet' with whom she corresponds under a false name – 'a Delia or a Celia, I assure you'. Notice how incidentally a good plot seems to develop. The threat of Bob Acres is raised and dismissed with the word 'odious'; finally, by means of this circuitous route, Lydia returns to Beverley. She tells Julia of an anonymous letter she wrote to herself, revealing the existence of 'another woman'; this she presented to Beverley in the hope of provoking a true lovers' quarrel, and vowed that she 'would never see him more'. Julia, with more mature insight, taxes Lydia with caprice, only to find herself having to defend Faulkland against the same charge, in words that leave us with the impression that he is not only capricious but intensely demanding.

Mrs Malaprop and Sir Anthony enter, to find Miss Languish the scholar sitting very upright and perusing a large volume of Chesterfield's letters. Perhaps she has turned to the page on which the Earl warns his son against the practice of laughing, even in private.

After a brief altercation, Mrs Malaprop, in spite of her misuse of words, manages to convey her strong distaste for Lydia's 'violent memories', and to send her to her room. Lydia's exit is positively defiant. After pursuing various topics of conversation, chosen by Sheridan to elicit the most predictable social attitudes, the 'old folk' come to an agreement as to the management of Lydia's meeting with Capt. Absolute; Sir Anthony gives an ominous demonstration of his concept of parental discipline: 'If she rejects this proposal, clap her under lock and key', and leaves.

The next matter to occupy Mrs Malaprop's mind is her amorous intrigue – as she hopes – with Sir Lucius O'Trigger. Believing herself incapable of being deceived by such a simpleton as Lucy, she orders the servant to attend on her soon, when she will give her another letter for Sir Lucius. When Mrs Malaprop has left, Lucy 'alters her manner', and drops the mask of simpleton to reveal her own conniving features. She is playing all parties off against each other. The final words of the speech add colour to the portrait of Sir Lucius: 'I found he had too much pride and deli- cacy to sacrifice the feelings of a gentleman to the necessities of his fortune'. By the time he appears, we shall recognise him.

Commentary

A typical dressing-room of the time would not be hard to recreate on the modern stage. Feminine ornaments, lace, delicately bound volumes, some English landscape paintings, and a few pieces of furniture upholstered according to Mrs Malaprop's taste rather than Lydia's, perhaps a chandelier hung from the flies: these can be used to create immediately the atmos- phere of Lydia's place of confinement; it is like a hothouse, a perfect place in which to languish, which is precisely what Lydia is doing at the start of the scene, surrounded by some degree of disarray, mirroring her lack of concentration and her restlessness.

The exchange about novels between Lucy and Lydia arises directly out of Lydia's character and situation. The titles are a mixture of the better fiction of the day (*Humphry Clinker* and *Peregrine Pickle* by Tobias Smollett) together with the most sentimental (*The Delicate Distress* by Elizabeth Griffith and *The Fatal Connection* by Mrs Fogerty). The more serious books in Lydia's possession are used, it would seem, for curling papers, for pressing, or merely for effect. By means of the book titles, Sheridan illuminates Lydia's inner world, which is a veritable clutter of fantasy and romantic ideas. We realise that before she can marry Capt. Absolute, she will have to undergo some kind of maturing process. This impression is heightened by her demand for sal volatile; these smelling salts were a common antidote to boredom or the spleen, that most prevalent eighteenth-century complaint.

A critical problem is posed by Julia's long speech about Faulkland. How is an audience or reader expected to respond to it? There is undoubtedly humour in the writing; every time she is forced to admit to Faulkland's weaknesses, she excuses them on account of his sensitive nature. Yet she must not be endowed with Lydia's emotional mannerisms, nor can she be so serious as to be dull. Julia's heroism consists of the delightful mixture of common sense and powerful love. Yet she too has to grow during the course of the play, so what is her nature lacking at this point? Perhaps she has to learn to be herself in the face of Faulkland's pursuit of the ideal woman.

The dialogue between Sir Anthony and Mrs Malaprop is something of a set piece. Circulating libraries and female education provoke the two personalities in the extreme, and provide a fertile breeding-ground for malapropisms; there have to be plenty of these soon after Mrs Malaprop's first appearance, so that the audience's ear can be properly attuned to them. By the time her speech draws to its end; 'I don't think there is a superstitious article in it', the linguistic confusion in Mrs Malaprop's mind has won from us our delight as well as our ridicule.

When a scene becomes almost static, as it does in this instance, it is usually because the playwright is intent on adding detail to his characters and the world they inhabit rather than on engendering comic incident. Do you think there is too much talk in Act I, scene ii? What will a modern audience find hard to follow, and what should be cut? You should not dismiss any of the dialogue as boring until, first, you have fully understood it, and then clearly imagined it in the context of a performance. Lucy's delving into her pockets for the books, for instance, and Lydia's physical posing, as well as all sorts of expansive gestures between the old folk, keep the eye occupied, and are inherent in the text itself.

Right from the start observe how Sheridan treats exits and entrances. The entrance of a new character in a scene is never incidental: it advances the action and draws focus to the actor coming on to the stage in a way that is alien to much modern writing. Consider Mrs Malaprop's opening sentence and Lydia's final challenge. The one tells us immediately the sort of she-dragon with whom the lovers will have to contend, the other comes close to asking for a round of applause. Sir Anthony is also given an exit line that invites audience response because of its outrageousness, while Mrs Malaprop's 'and your being a simpleton shall be no excuse for your locality' ought to provoke a laugh to cover an otherwise weak exit. For a young man claiming to be ignorant of plays, Sheridan was no mean craftsman.

Lucy's soliloquy provides further evidence of this. It enables her to develop a special relationship with the audience; she may be a little villainess, but she has taken us into her confidence, and that affords an added perspective to the action when she is on stage.

Act II, Scene i

Summary

At Capt. Absolute's lodgings, Fag informs his master of Sir Anthony's presence in Bath; he explains that, in order to protect him from his father's suspicions, he has lied, maintaining that they are in Bath on a recruiting campaign.

The scene between Faulkland and Jack clarifies their respective relationships with Julia and Lydia, and allows us to see the great difference between the two men; the ensuing encounter between them and Bob Acres succeeds in rousing Faulkland to a peak of jealousy owing to Bob's inane chatter about Julia's dancing and high spirits. When Acres and Absolute are left alone, the country boohy reveals his intention to pursue fashion so as to obtain Lydia; he explains the nature of 'sentimental swearing', and mentions his desire to contact Sir Lucius.

The last part of the scene shows us Sir Anthony's complete intransigence in the matter of marrying off his son.

Commentary

Capt. Absolute stands before us, at his lodgings. His red coat is almost startling. From all we have heard, we expect to find him a dashing, inventive young officer, deeply in love but besieged by Lydia's expectations. We are not disappointed, though he does seem very down to earth in comparison with Lydia's portrait of him.

All through this scene, as with the previous one, we can see Sheridan working to avoid too obvious a development of plot and character. A speech starts with an incidental topic that leads on to more important matter. For instance, Faulkland's melancholy reply to Absolute's invitation to dine is the cue for a bout of teasing that leads Faulkland to express his inmost concerns. He, like Lydia, is a victim of his own theories of love, which owe more to literature than to life: 'If it rains, some shower may even then have chilled her delicate frame. If the wind be keen, some rude blast may have affected her.' Such sentiments arise, not from the possibility of natural disasters, but from an overheated imagination. With the arrival of Bob Acres, Absolute has two friends to tease; he stage-manages the scene, encouraging Acres to tread on Faulkland's toes. We share Absolute's amusement as we watch Faulkland developing emotional indigestion that worsens whenever Acres opens his mouth, oblivious to the effect he is having. We love both of them for their gullibility, and are perhaps a little glad that we are not in a position to be the target of Jack's military humour.

After Faulkland has left in a rage – which Acres completely misunderstands – we find out more about Acres himself, and about his pretensions to fashion, and it is out of this conversation that there arises, again apparently incidentally, a more important matter:

> ABSOLUTE   Oh, you'll polish, I doubt not.
> ACRES   Absolutely I propose so – then if I can find out this Ensign Beverley, odds triggers and flints! I'll make him know the difference o't.

At one stroke, Sheridan has prepared us for the eventual confrontation between these two friends, and has made us aware that only such a confrontation will be able to strip Acres of his pretension.

Sir Anthony's entrance is timed perfectly. We had almost forgotten about him, and his approach is like that of a thundercloud. He cannot mention the name of the young lady he intends as his son's bride, of course, or the whole basis for misunderstanding on which the play depends will be removed; his character justifies such reserve. Notice how Sir Anthony introduces the topic of marriage as though it is of secondary importance, perhaps while searching for his snuff-box or adjusting his wig; he delivers the good news that he's intending to confer a fortune on Jack, and then:

> ABSOLUTE   Yet, Sir, I presume you would not wish me to quit the army?
> SIR ANT.   Oh, that shall be as your wife chooses.
> ABSOLUTE   My wife, Sir!

As Jack argues his case with increasing vehemence, the audience is aware that he is arguing against his own interests, but we take delight in the complications that we anticipate. When he takes a stand with 'my inclinations are fixed on another', and declines to marry the 'mass of ugliness' he imagines his father has in store for him, his declaration of disobedience provokes his father into unmasking his absoluteness:

> Zounds! Sirrah! the lady shall be as ugly as I choose: she shall have a lump on each shoulder; she shall be as crooked as the crescent; her one eye shall roll like the bull's in Cox's Museum.

We can now see him as Jack does: a gouty old tyrant, and we warm to

Jack as we see him bearing the attack with filial patience, if not obedience. However, once his father has left, Jack takes out his temper on Fag, who in his turn rounds on the errand boy; physical repercussions of this kind are a simple way of integrating a household!

This is a long scene, and not a strikingly active one, the emphasis being largely on character and on the interaction of contrasting types. Fag is shown to have the flexible conscience of a servant who will do anything to get his master, and himself, out of a scrape; he regards lying as part of his job, but draws the line at being found out. Faulkland suffers from a fashionable form of melancholia, Sir Anthony from believing that he's never in the wrong, and Bob from the desire to be what he can never be. We are invited to inspect lovingly these peculiarities of nature as if under a magnifying glass; we laugh, partly because the detail is so consistent, and partly because everyone apart from Jack lacks self-knowledge to a greater or lesser extent. Lack of self-knowledge leads to rigidity of character and, as Henri Bergson said, 'This rigidity is the comic, and laughter is its corrective'.

Act II, Scene ii

Summary
Lucy gives Sir Lucius a letter from his Delia, which he believes has come from Lydia. 'Experience! what, at seventeen?' With these words Sir Lucius betrays that he has been quite taken in by Lucy's ploy. He talks of Mrs Malaprop as 'the old gentlewoman', and sees her as a necessary evil where his dear Delia is concerned. Once he has read the letter out loud and somewhat marvelled at its language, the implications of which elude him, he leaves, inflated with optimism. Fag enters suddenly; clearly he has been spying. He thinks his master may have been betrayed, but Lucy laughs at him and reveals that the letter she gave Sir Lucius came from Mrs Malaprop. With mistaken triumph in her voice, Lucy tells Fag, whom she knows as Ensign Beverley's servant, that 'Sir Anthony has proposed his son' for Lydia's hand. Fag's 'ha! ha! ha!' is not the reaction for which she had hoped.

Commentary
The external location of this scene makes it brighter than it at first appears on the page; even so, some of the writing is a little heavy-handed. Malapropisms at second-hand – that is, in the letter read out by Sir Lucius – seem half-hearted by comparison with those spoken by the inventor. Sheridan seems to take extra pains to ensure that we understand and believe the situation, whereas we are probably willing to take it on trust. However, the scene introduces us to Sir Lucius and to his mercenary

motive for seeking to marry. We can guess that he too is doomed to a comic downfall when the truth becomes apparent.

Act III, Scene i

Summary
Since this scene is set in the same location as the last one and yet is separate from it, Sheridan probably had an interval and entr'acte in mind between the two. This means that at the beginning of the second half, all the strands of the plot are twisted tight; now we have to watch how they will interweave and unravel.

Clearly, Fag has informed his master of what Lucy said: 'My father wants to force me to marry the very girl I am plotting to run away with.' He has caught up with us and shares our sense of irony. His father's arrival makes him resort to his acting talents. He has decided that the only safe way of dealing with the situation is to pretend to be willing to marry Lydia Languish, solely for the sake of pleasing his father.

Sir Anthony enters, muttering and spluttering that he will never see his son again, only to be stopped dead in his tracks by seeing a 'penitential face' and hearing a resolution of obedience. He is immediately all smiles himself. There follows a cleverly written exchange, with Sir Anthony trying to arouse Jack's interest in Lydia, while Jack, with some difficulty, pretends a complete lack of interest, even to the point of being willing to marry Mrs Malaprop, should his father prefer that arrangement, so that the old man can marry Lydia himself. Sir Anthony is flabbergasted, for the Absolutes have ever been a manly stock and are not meant to be impervious to feminine charms – as long as they coincide with the paternal choice! Jack, for his part, dare not reveal the truth, because Sir Anthony would undoubtedly do a swift about-turn or, worse, ruin all by 'too summary a method of proceeding'. Above all, he has to try to preserve Lydia from too rude an awakening.

Sir Anthony is driven by Jack's performance to command exactly what Jack desires: 'I'll write a note to Mrs Malaprop, and you shall visit the lady directly.' The exit needs something extra. Does Jack throw a discreet glance at the audience? Or is there music to bridge the scenes?

Commentary
This short scene is a masterly piece of comic writing: economical and precise; it relies heavily on a single joke, but explores all the implications of it. You need to identify with Jack in his dilemma to find out quite how well the scene is constructed. The more emotional he forces his father to become in painting the pleasures of young love, the cooler Jack

plays it. This is the secret behind most of the laughter the scene provokes. Look, for instance, at these consecutive lines:

SIR ANT.   Then, Jack, her neck. O Jack! Jack!
ABSOLUTE   And which is to be mine, Sir, the niece or the aunt?

or these:

SIR ANT.   ... when I ran away with your mother, I would not have touched anything old or ugly to gain an empire.
ABSOLUTE   Not to please your father, Sir?
SIR ANT.   To please my father! Zounds! not to please – O my father! – odso! – yes – yes!

The scene naturally reaches its climax when Sir Anthony showers his son with insults, calling him a sot, a block, a hypocrite and a liar. Once he has given vent to his fury, Sir Anthony is able to clear the path for action: 'you shall visit the lady directly'. Jack obviously knows his father's temper very well, as Sheridan knew *his* father's, so he fuels it to make sure they both go in the right direction.

Act III, Scene ii

Summary
In Julia's dressing-room, Faulkland, alone, reproves himself for his capriciousness; but as soon as Julia enters, he gives way to it again. He berates and insults her, each insult, as he believes, being a gentle means of awakening his beloved to the high and demanding duties of love. He goes so far as to question the integrity of her heart, fearing that her feelings for him may in reality be no more than gratitude – he did, after all, save her from drowning. He responds to Julia's obvious suffering with the neurotic paradox, 'If I loved you less, I should never give you an uneasy moment.' The problem is, he never gives her an easy one. It is not surprising that Sheridan decides to send her out of the room in tears.

In a flurry of remorse, Faulkland calls after her; begs forgiveness; then chastises her with lack of charity and himself with lack of manliness; gives way to a passionate determination not to distress her again, and absurdly invites retribution on his head, should he do so. It is noticeable that in the middle of the soliloquy, when he thinks Julia is returning, he denounces her for doing so: 'She is coming too – I thought she would – no steadiness in anything!' His last lines, invoking the curse of an 'antique virago' on himself if he ever distresses Julia again, are positively operatic and, given the tone of the play, they undermine his own solemnity. We do not expect Faulkland to be able to carry out his resolution because almost every time he has opened his mouth during the scene, he has convicted himself of a comic obsession, which will need a powerful shock to dislodge it.

Commentary

This is the first Faulkland/Julia scene. Sheridan has left it quite late in the play to start exploring their relationship.

This scene and its partner (V.i.) cause more problems of interpretation than almost anything in eighteenth-century comedy. A modern reader or audience member is prepared for Faulkland's outburst, stemming from his exaggerated idealism; what most of us are not prepared for, particularly in today's climate of feminism, is the extent to which Julia makes allowances for his methods of mental torture; nor are we prepared, I think, for the length of the scene. Has Sheridan misjudged its entertainment value? Has he become so subtle in his reproduction of sentimental comedy that he has in fact created something too close to the original to be amusing? That is a common hazard for the parodist or satirist. Or did Sheridan intend us to take the scene quite seriously, to delight us with subtle affections and romantic doubts? Maybe the answer is a mixture of all these. No matter how sincere or ingenious the actors, there will always be critics who will react to Faulkland's horrified 'In tears', with the thought that he is an ass, and not nearly good enough for Julia; they will never believe her good nature could allow itself to be so besieged. Well, that is partly a question of contemporary attitudes being imposed on the play, and frequently it is partly the result of the actors being unable to hit quite the right note. Faulkland should be an infuriating, yet endearing sight, as he twists and turns in the grip of his own obsession. It might be illuminating for a group to read part of the scene aloud, once as comedy, and once as tragedy. You may find the second reading funnier than the first.

Act III, Scene iii

Summary

Mrs Malaprop interviews Capt. Absolute at her lodgings. This scene is the result of Sir Anthony's decision at the end of III.i.; the letter in Mrs Malaprop's hand as she enters is the one he promised to write on his son's behalf. Mrs Malaprop begins by denouncing Ensign Beverley and all his works, including his liaison with Lydia; Jack, tongue firmly in cheek, enthusiastically agrees with her, secure in the knowledge that his dual identity is a secret. When Lydia comes down, under duress and at Mrs Malaprop's behest, to meet her suitor, Jack declares that he, i.e. Beverley, has come pretending to be Capt. Absolute. Are you having a little difficulty remembering precisely who knows what about whom? That is part of the fun.

When Mrs Malaprop re-enters, she misinterprets a sentimental wooing scene Jack has stage-managed in order to lull Lydia with dreams of love and poverty; the tough old aunt sees and hears a Lydia full of defiance and rebellion! She drags the young girl protesting from the room, and repeating the name 'Beverley' like a battle-cry.

Commentary

The two duologues that compose the bulk of the scene are a beautiful exploration of the muddle produced by Jack's false identity; Mrs Malaprop knows who he is but doesn't know who he is pretending to be; Lydia knows who he is pretending to be, but doesn't know that he is pretending. Jack is caught between the two, and his main aim is to convince each one of what she thinks she knows, without letting the wrong information enter the wrong ear ('gently, good tongue'). To Mrs Malaprop he makes himself appear a champion in her cause against the impertinent Beverley; to Lydia he out-Beverleys all former performances of Beverley in a reckless parody of the language he judges suitable for his adopted persona:

> Proud of calamity, we will enjoy the wreck of wealth, while the surrounding gloom of adversity shall make the flame of our pure love show doubly bright.

The brief unit of the scene during which Mrs Malaprop eavesdrops, misinterprets what she observes, and then advances like an avenging angel to take Lydia to task for her rude behaviour, is another fine piece of comic writing; but once again it depends on physical as well as verbal humour, and it is not an easy moment to stage. Perhaps Mrs Malaprop hides behind flats as she moves further downstage. Or maybe she stands behind a screen, like Lady Teazle in *The School for Scandal*. Maybe she stands in the open, but some way upstage, behind Lydia and Jack. Whichever way the director chooses, there is a problem in timing Mrs Malaprop's interjections and in making them audible but not so loud that we think Mrs Malaprop must inevitably overhear Lydia and Jack. Conventions of delivering asides, available to Sheridan and his actors, have been modified in our own day for the sake of credibility. As the scene is read, one should try to imagine what the other two characters are doing to fill the moments when Mrs Malaprop is expostulating. Surely they cannot form tableaux, for these are alien to the realistic style in which the play is written?

The end of the scene leaves a momentarily triumphant Capt. Absolute 'kissing his hand' to the departing Lydia, but he is aware that he is in an increasingly tight spot: there is no doubt that ultimately the 'old folk' are in command; if he is to escape from the mesh he himself has woven, he will have to do so by cooperation, not elopement! This is the sub-text beneath the kissing of the hand.

Act III, Scene iv

Summary
At Acres' lodgings we find the country booby transformed unconvincingly into a man of fashion. He is all spruced up, with his new curls and his new clothes, and is convinced that he now looks like a member of the highest society, and killingly handsome at that. David, his servant from Clod Hall, is sceptical about such polishing, and obviously finds it inappropriate to his master's personality. When Acres is left on his own, he practises his cotillon (*sic*), an eighteenth-century dance chosen by Sheridan to show Acres at his most galumphing. He's a man in the wrong world, but unlike Faulkland's, his vanity threatens no one but himself.

Sir Lucius notices no finery. He comes straight to the point: 'A rival in the case, is there? And you think he has supplanted you unfairly?'

As soon as the word 'rival' is in the air, bullets are liable to fly, if Sir Lucius O'Trigger is around. He begins to direct the forthcoming drama, and to arouse Acres' spirit to revenge: 'Can a man commit a more heinous offence against another man than to fall in love with the same woman?' He works Acres up into a lather, so that he is emotionally prepared for a duel, though, like Sir Andrew Aguecheek in Shakespeare's *Twelfth Night*, he is obviously incapable of going through with it.

Acres is persuaded by false arguments, and by appeals to examples drawn from the classical world and Blunderbuss Hall. He must send a challenge to Ensign Beverley to meet him in King's Mead Fields; Sir Lucius meanwhile (and in this aspect of the plot Sheridan is less careful than usual about credibility) is to go in search of 'a gay captain here, who put a jest on me lately, at the expense of my country'. We know who that must be. Bully O'Trigger and boasting Acres are both looking for a fight with Jack.

Commentary
The plot begins to thicken, but in the latter stages of the scene the author is in danger of making it curdle. The early part is well constructed: the brief scene between Bob, parading his attire, and David, commenting with rustic insight which fails to penetrate Acres' vanity; then Bob's soliloquy, which offers an actor the chance to explore the essence of his character and to draw closer to the audience; most of the scene with Sir Lucius is extremely funny – the call to vengeance, the example of Blunderbuss Hall, and particularly the writing of the challenge in formal terms dictated by Sir Lucius. It is in the concocting of a reason for Sir Lucius to

seek a duel with Absolute that the jarring note occurs. Irish jokes were probably common enough, but since we don't witness the confrontation, we find it hard to accept, I think, as anything more than a device to move the plot in the direction the playwright requires. However, Sheridan finishes the scene confidently with Sir Lucius's line 'Let your courage be as keen, but at the same time as polished as your sword.' There is in the line an unmistakable rhythm, one that seems to beat in the very heart of O'Trigger of Blunderbuss Hall.

Act IV, Scene i

Summary
David and Acres argue about how far concepts of honour should be allowed to steer one's life. Absolute arrives to find his friend thundering (if Acres can be said to thunder) at his faithful servant because of his cowardice. Acres thrusts the freshly penned challenge at the man it's intended for – though, of course, he doesn't know that – and asks him to deliver the 'mortal defiance'. Absolute accepts the task, but declines to appear as his friend's second; he has to, because he's going to appear as his opponent. A servant informs Absolute that his father is waiting for him, but Jack cannot get out of the door before Acres has begged him to tell Beverley that he will be up against 'a devil of a fellow'.

Commentary
An interval of about five minutes was customary after each act, but before this scene there is a practical need for one, is there not?

David has as little time for the battle cries of an old blunderbuss like Sir Lucius as he has for the exquisite culture of his master's curls. Honour is all very well, so long as it doesn't require one to lie down and die for it. His philosophy owes something to Falstaff's in Shakespeare's *Henry IV, Part I*:

> . . . Can honour set-to a leg? no: or an arm? no: or take away the grief of a wound? no. What is honour? a word. What is in that word, honour? What is that honour? air. A trim reckoning! – Who hath it? he that died o'Wednesday. Doth he feel it? no. Doth he hear it? no. Is it insensible, then? yea, to the dead. But will it not live with the living? no.

David argues to dilute Acres' courage, just as Sir Lucius had taken pains to strengthen it. He is nearly as successful. Even his 'whimpering' is aimed as a deterrent, and by invoking the names of Clod Hall, Phillis his dog, and Old Crop his horse, he comes near to making his master whimper as well; then Jack arrives.

The end of this scene, as of the last, is rather contrived. Sheridan seems to be relying on the mounting tension and bustle to make the challenge business acceptable; he allows the audience little time to think. The very last moments of the scene need some physical action if they are not to fall flat. Perhaps Acres skirmishes in a mirror with an imaginary sword, and then retreats from his own image in fright.

Act IV, Scene ii

Summary
At Mrs Malaprop's lodgings, the Absolute/Lydia seam of the plot erupts from fantasy into truth.

It begins by extending the basic joke of split identity, as Mrs Malaprop praises Captain Absolute in glowing terms; Lydia laughs, knowing perfectly well that her aunt has been grossly deceived and is talking about her dear Beverley.

When a servant informs the ladies that Sir Anthony and Capt. Absolute are below, Lydia 'flings herself into a chair, with her face from the door', ensuring that she won't have to look at the foolish face of Beverley's rival, even on his entering the room.

What follows is close to farce. Absolute has to avoid speaking loud enough for Lydia to recognise his voice; if the truth comes to light under these circumstances, both Lydia and his father will probably treat him like a scoundrel. Sir Anthony is prodding him to action with his cane; Jack is forced to expostulate in a disguised voice. There is a deadlock: Mrs Malaprop is unable to get Lydia to turn round, while Sir Anthony cannot get Jack to make intelligible overtures. Jack pretends to make an effort – 'Hem! hem! madam – hem!' – a very feeble effort. He has a moment of hope, when Mrs Malaprop suggests that she and Sir Anthony withdraw; but the suspicious Sir Anthony refuses, and Jack has once more to approach the adored back. He speaks in a 'low, hoarse tone': 'Will not Miss Languish lend an ear to the mild accents of true love?' His father's temper is fraying. Mrs Malaprop, aghast at Lydia's lack of decorum, attempts to turn her round; as she chides Jack takes the desperate decision to reveal the truth.

This produces further complications. Jack's confession that his identity as Beverley was only assumed for 'the singular benefit of her temper' meets with the tragic reproach: 'So! – there will be no elopement after all!'

Sir Anthony is delighted by the discovery that his son is by no means the milksop he had pretended to be. Mrs Malaprop, on the other hand, has had the wind taken out of her sails, realising that it was her hero himself who referred to her by 'the elegant compilation of an old, weather-beaten she-dragon!' Sir Anthony acts as peacemaker, and gaily exits with the pacified dragon in tow. The young couple are left by themselves.

Lydia is sitting unapproachably in her chair again, facing away from Jack. Her hands are reclining, ominously still, in her lap. By talking of friends' consent, lawyers, and the licence, Jack is offending Lydia's romantic ear. For her, all has suddenly become grey and dull as legal parchment. She turns on him with surprising spirit; she flings his miniature at him, and renounces him for ever from her heart. He is not to be outdone, at least he thinks he isn't. He reverses the accusations, produces her miniature from round his neck. . .but has not the gall to throw it on the ground as she did.

Jack's final weapon is his sharpest: 'Or perhaps, they may be ill-natured enough to hint, that the gentleman grew tired of the lady and forsook her.' This wounds her vanity and brings her to a halt. Maybe she has wafted across the room and is now perched uncomfortably on a stool; she has no answer but a stare, then a cascade of tears.

Further misunderstandings are in store for poor Jack. When Sir Anthony and Mrs Malaprop return, they find no billing and cooing, but sobbing and sullenness; with a public renunciation, Lydia sweeps out, to misery – and, one suspects, after being inconsolable for a few minutes, to tea. Sir Anthony, immediately followed by Mrs Malaprop, jumps to the conclusion that Jack has 'behaved disrespectfully', behaved 'too lively' towards Lydia. The proud father chortles merrily to find his son such a rogue, such a thorough Absolute. Jack tries in vain to protest, for Sir Anthony will have none of it: 'It runs in the blood of our family', he proclaims, and delegates Mrs Malaprop to make peace between the young couple.

Commentary

One of the mistakes that a modern reader or audience member can make is that of confusing fine manners with superciliousness, or acting with posing. This confusion can lead to the view that all the characters are equally artificial, and that their true emotions never show above the social glaze. Nothing could be further from the truth. Jack's antics in this scene stem from very real emotions indeed; his love is real, so is his desire to escape from the present trap. Lydia's anguish is immature, but deeply felt. Sir Anthony's intolerance is more a matter of feeling than anything else, as are Mrs Malaprop's indignation and embarrassment. It is most important that we recognise these emotions for what they are, or the world of the play will become arid and unattractive; when even professional actors fail to differentiate between foppery and high style, between embellishment and true wit, the whole play is distorted.

A word about wit. In Restoration comedy, the possession of wit was a necessity for the young hero, the man about town. Wit was regarded as the highest intellectual virtue; it consisted, at one level, of saying the cleverest things in the best possible way at exactly the right moment, and, at another, of being well-versed in all the arts suitable to be studied by an English gentleman. The greatest of these arts was naturally that of coping with the opposite sex. The fop aimed at wit, but fell short through a lack of self-knowledge or a certain vulgarity of mind.

In *The Rivals* there are traces of all these social criteria, though they have been greatly diminished in accordance with the taste of an age which required of its hero more sincerity and less wit. Jack, though, bears some resemblance to Dorimant (from Sir George Etherege's *The Man of Mode*) and Mirabell (from William Congreve's *The Way of the World*), leading wits of the drama of the previous age, in that he is rarely at a loss for the appropriate word or the appropriate action. In IV.ii. our delight is increased by watching one who is usually so in control, both of himself and of the situation, floundering ridiculously; Jack becomes more human and more likeable the more events overtake him. This feature too he has inherited from his more ribald predecessors.

In the summary of this scene, its physical aspects were particularly stressed. More than almost any other scene in the play, it requires staging to bring out its humour, and the vocal effects are as much needed in this respect as the visual; one has only to imagine Jack 'croaking like a frog in a quinsy' to realise this. Much of the fun in the earlier part of the scene derives from Sheridan making a virtue of necessity. Lydia cannot be allowed to see Capt. Absolute, or the game will be up. By facing her away from her beloved, the playwright extracts every ounce of comedy from the situation. We don't find it contrived, because character and action are so well blended.

Jack's persona of the youth embarrassed by the charms of a young lady probably owes something to Goldsmith's character Marlowe in *She Stoops to Conquer* (1773). There may even be an element of conscious imitation, which the audience were expected to enjoy.

Although it is early in the play for the hero's identity trick to be revealed, the truth sets off a further series of complications, because Lydia cannot yet face it.

Act IV, Scene iii

Summary

Sir Lucius walks on to the North Parade, swearing about Capt. Absolute, and the latter walks on from the other side, cursing about Lydia. The Irishman confronts the Englishman, intent on a duel; Jack, feeling hurt and rejected, is himself in a fighting mood. He agrees to meet Sir Lucius a little after six o'clock in King's Mead Fields. We suffer with our hero in his frustration, as he fails to make any sense of Sir Lucius's challenge, and it only increases with Faulkland's entrance. In answer to Jack's attempt to enlist him as a second, his self-centred friend can only cite his own unease at his recent, cruel treatment of Julia. 'Enter servant, gives Faulkland a letter, and exits.' A charmingly easy way of advancing a plot! The contents of Julia's letter are forgiving and generous, yet even now Faulkland has a fit of the scruples: ' . . . own honestly – don't you think the there is something forward, something indelicate in this haste to forgive?'

Jack's patience finally bursts; his righteous indignation is real and his words are harsh: Faulkland is in his eyes 'a subject more fit for ridicule than compassion', but they are those of a friend pushed beyond his limit, not of suddenly discovered enmity.

Faulkland's reaction is so predictable that it is almost surprising! He acknowledges the justice behind Jack's accusation that he is 'a slave to fretfulness and whim' but congratulates himself on this as being the sign of a superior temperament. Forgetting his earlier intentions of recon-ciliation, he confides in us that he is about to use the forthcoming duel to test Julia's sincerity one last time. 'The silly ass!' we think, 'He'll spoil everything' – as he nearly does. Once again, the consciously 'heroic' exit gives him away.

Commentary
Sir Lucius's soliloquy does little to fill out his character, though the passing reference to Lady Dorothy Carmine certainly reminds us of his social pretensions and of his almost professional pursuit of a dowry. It is also clear that, national jokes or no, his real grudge against Absolute has to do with women. Technically speaking, Sheridan needs the soliloquy to enable Absolute to arrive on the North Parade, without depositing him there straight from Mrs Malaprop's.

Although the scene does not entirely lack humour, mostly created by Sir Lucius's unwillingness to define his motives for the challenge, yet there is a sour note in the dialogue not heard before, and a real threat in the attitude of Sir Lucius. Sheridan shows Absolute under strain and not quite able to overcome the effects of circumstance with a show of his normal bravura.

Servants in eighteenth-century comedy are numerous, and can be used for any of the functions they would carry out in real life. That does not mean, however, that the actor playing the servant need allow his moment to slip by, completely unnoticed. Perhaps the servant who hands Julia's letter to Faulkland could be one of those solemn, liveried types, and extremely disapproving of Faulkland – who has probably upset the whole household with his delays. Alternatively, could it be the coachman, who has been hurriedly dispatched?

Every actor knows that he has to search for the key to his character, not only in his relationships with others, nor simply in his own speeches, but in what is said about him. An actor preparing to play Faulkland might do well to start with what Jack, giving vent to truth in a moment of anger, says to his friend:

> Confound your buts. You never hear anything that would make another man bless himself, but you immediately damn it with a but.

Act V, Scene i

Summary

Faulkland's final test of Julia succeeds only in driving them apart. In acting the role of the banished hero and then as suddenly discarding it, he goes too far, even for Julia's patience. She reproves him with the deepest feeling. Faulkland is indeed stricken, yet he cannot escape from his self-dramatising; as he heads off in the direction of King's Mead Fields, he sees himself as a victim of love, as a ready sacrifice in a duel, but still as one of the 'subtler spirits'.

Julia re-enters, composing herself after her encounter with Faulkland, to find Lydia, typically waiting to regale her with the latest tale of woe, in which potential rags have changed to despised riches. Oh, all the dreams, the ecstatic moments, the 'dripping statue' – and now, after all that, there will be 'a bishop's licence', her 'aunt's blessing' and 'simpering up to the altar': just an ordinary wedding! All has become prosaic and horrible. Julia, in a few lines that echo Jack's words to Faulkland at the end of Act IV, scene ii, begs Lydia not to give way to caprice or to reject one who truly loves her. At this moment, Sheridan explicitly links the love-matches, by showing that romantic folly is the cause of the present unhappiness of both couples.

After the static quality of the scene up to this point, Sheridan asks us to take a breath, and then urges the action towards its extended climax. Mrs Malaprop enters, firing off in all directions about an impending 'antistrophe'; Fag and David follow her; the first confuses and delays matters by trying to deliver a eulogy, in high style, about Capt. Absolute; the second blurts out something of what is going on in the Fields. All the ladies have a man at stake, even Mrs Malaprop, for she has heard that they have 'drawn poor little dear Sir Lucius into the scrape'. They are away at once, with Fag leading and David urging them on from behind.

Commentary

Julia's tone in this scene is so serious – she is such an unwary victim of Faulkland's final test – that it is hard to extract the comedy that is undoubtedly there. Once he has thrown off his disguise, however, there is no room for joking. If you study Julia's long speech, beginning, 'As my faith has once been given to you, I never will barter it for another', you will find that the prose she is given to speak is rhythmic and fluent. The force of her anguish has broken simultaneously through Faulkland's armoured exterior and through the web of comedy, both 'sentimental' and 'laughing'. We are faced with very real feelings in Faulkland's contrived situation, and the experience is painful, not just for Julia but for us as well. This speech, and the sudden deepening effect it has on the play, manifests Sheridan's genius as much as the funniest moments.

Lydia's character, as with the others, defines itself most clearly at the moment of highest distress. Her exquisite picture of what she thought love to be, is at the heart of the problem.

Mrs Malaprop's entrance at the end of the scene should be like the boosting of a rocket: a sudden lift in energy and excitement. Since we have no doubt at all that everyone will survive King's Mead Fields, we watch the events leading up to the duel with delighted detachment. Confusion among characters on stage is sometimes a great aid to clarity among the audience, and so it is here. It provides us with the opportunity to confirm that Lydia and Julia are by no means finished with their respective suitors, even though they may have said as much; Sheridan gives the girls few lines at the end of the scene, because he knows their agitated silence will be more eloquent. And where is David, once he has delivered his news?

Act V, Scene ii

Summary
Absolute comes on to the South Parade, trying to hide his forbidden sword under his greatcoat. He is waiting for Faulkland, his second, but instead sees his father coming. He escapes from Sir Anthony by means of comic voices and white lies about where he is going and what he is doing with a sword under his coat, then races away to fight Sir Lucius, or Bob Acres, or (one feels at this stage) anyone else who wishes to pick a quarrel with him.

David rushes on, shouting 'murder' and 'slaughter'; Sir Anthony stops him in his tracks by calling him a 'dunce', and gets the facts out of him. Furious at having been deceived by Jack, he seizes David's shoulder in order to take the weight off his gouty foot, and off they march to King's Mead Fields, Sir Anthony, no doubt, brandishing his stick.

Commentary
Jack's disguising of his voice is amusing, and the sword-business, though a little laboured, provides a moment of hilarity. But do we not find that

there is something unsatisfactory about it all? Captain Absolute's dark mood matches ill with the comic antics to which he is obliged to resort. One tends to feel that one is watching a replay of the previous scene between father and son, on the North Parade (III.i.), and it seems too late in the play for such incidental humour to be given so prominent a place. One can see that the scene is structurally necessary and has been kept as brief as possible.

David's entrance is a booster, like Mrs Malaprop's in the previous scene, and it provides the cue for all to converge on King's Mead Fields.

Act V, Scene iii

Summary
We have reached King's Mead Fields, where Sir Lucius is trying to prepare Acres to do battle, while the latter, visibly trembling in his tight breeches, would obviously rather run all the way home to Clod Hall than fight Ensign Beverley. He does not take kindly to the idea of being 'pickled and sent home' or of 'snug lying in the Abbey'. By the time Faulkland and Absolute enter, he has been wrought to a state of abject terror, and would definitely take to his heels but for Sir Lucius's eagle eye and his persistent reminders of the call to Honour.

What now happens between the four men is complicated, and although on stage the confusion and speed of events adds to our amusement, the student should know exactly what is going on. Sheridan worked it out; there's no reason why we shouldn't. First of all, Sir Lucius mistakes Faulkland for Acres' opponent, Beverley. Acres disabuses Sir Lucius, claiming Faulkland as his friend. Sir Lucius, his blood up, wants a fight at any cost, and cordially invites Faulkland to fight Acres anyway. Faulkland, the ready victim, shows willing. Acres refuses the offer. Sir Lucius says he 'is not to be trifled with', but Acres replies that it was Beverley he challenged, and he will fight Beverley or no one. Jack steps in and announces the truth – that he is Beverley. 'Well, this is lucky – now you have an opportunity –', rejoices Sir Lucius, but 'Fighting Bob' won't countenance the idea of a duel with his old friend; besides, his legs have turned to jelly. Sir Lucius calls Acres a coward; this should, according to the code of honour, provoke a duel, but Acres can only bluster. The second duel on the cards, that between Absolute and Sir Lucius, begins in earnest.

The entrance of Sir Anthony and the others is the cue for a series of rapid unravellings. The cause of the duel is revealed; the Delia mystery, together with Mrs Malaprop's owning to that winsome title, is 'dissolved'. Absolute declares his enduring love for Lydia, and Faulkland and Julia are reconciled under the approving eye of Sir Anthony. Mrs Malaprop appears cast down, and both she and Bob are left 'unprovided for'; but the humiliation of the one and the deprivation of the other are necessary to the broadening out of the comedy, as evening closes on the action and we have a last moment to survey the assembled company.

The final speeches encapsulate the theme of the play and draw the audience into the serenity of a future unmarred by passion, and, one may infer, by Lydia's caprice or Faulkland's absurd demands.

Commentary
At the beginning of this scene, on the eighteenth-century stage, all flats would have been removed, and the area would have been left as open as possible. We need to feel that the action has moved outside the city.

The final scene of a Comedy of Manners, as of a Shakespearean comedy, has to make peace where there has been division, and to show the reconciled lovers firmly set on their path to marriage and happiness. Those who need to be brought down a peg or two receive their dues, and covert intrigues, in this case Lucy's, are exposed to the light of day.

The wrapping up of a play of this kind can be a synthetic business. Sometimes a playwright finds it necessary to introduce a fortuitous occurrence, by way of an unexpected inheritance or the arrival of a new character bearing good news. It is to Sheridan's credit that all he does is to reveal truths that have been concealed from the participants, though not from the spectators. We enjoy the privilege of spies, and our satisfaction at watching things turn out as they should do, is, therefore, the greater. Nor is the ending too neat and tidy to be believed; there are some loose ends and unanswered questions about what the future holds; and Mrs Malaprop's, 'Men are all barbarians' strikes a note that is not entirely harmonious. The play at its close does not congeal into uniform sentimentality.

The Epilogue
This presents a moral because the ladies demand one; so the writer, with his tongue firmly in his cheek, announces, and then proceeds to take as his theme the power of the female sex. Women rule their men folk, from statesmen seeking counsel, to the 'wand'ring tar' returned to his partner after a long absence; women smile preferment and frown disgrace, and when he hears his Nancy cry, the brave soldier's heart 'sickens at a tear'. On women the social happiness of the land depends. BUT - one hears a trace of Faulkland in the reservation - 'But ye more cautious - ye nice judging few': those who know the true value of beauty and charm know how to beware of them; ah, if only women were always reasonable!

> In female breasts did sense and merit rule,
> The lover's mind would ask no other school.

Since all the actors would have been present for the epilogue, it is hard to imagine that in the original production Mrs Bulkley, playing Julia, did not direct a glance during these lines at Miss Barsanti, playing Lydia Languish (to whom they so pertinently applied before her sudden reformation in the last scene) or that when they watched the play together, Sheridan did not glance at Eliza to see how she liked this moral.

4 THEMES AND ISSUES

Two separate issues in *The Rivals* integrate the play; the plot is inextricably bound up with them.

4.1 YOUNG AND OLD; THE ARRANGED MARRIAGE

The marriage of convenience, or the arranged marriage, was a commonplace theme for writers of Comedy of Manners. Often the playwright would show such a match in the worst possible light, and the father's choice of partner for his son or daughter would be extremely unsuitable. The best example of this occurs in *Tartuffe* (1664) by Molière: in this play Orgon insists on attempting to marry off his daughter to a man whom everyone else on the stage and in the audience regards as a hypocrite driven by greed and lust. Sheridan's plot twists this convention around, for Captain Absolute's anticipated 'mass of ugliness' turns out to be none other than Lydia herself. Nevertheless, many of the complications in the play do arise from the meddling of father and aunt with the affections of their respective charges. The institution of the arranged marriage is not a direct target for satire in this case, but the implications of the play are in favour of leaving young people to work out their own destinies. The battle between youth and age is fought largely over this issue. While the outcome is firmly on the side of youth, Sir Anthony's general goodwill and happiness at the end of the play balance this impression.

Much of the humour that is extracted from the encounters between young and old depends on tone and on the underlying assumptions on each side. The offhanded manner of Sir Anthony in the following lines is not only calculated to stop his son from flaring up, it accurately represents the way he thinks:

Yes, Jack, the independence I was talking of is by marriage – the
fortune is saddled with a wife – but I suppose that makes no
difference.

Mrs Malaprop's tone towards Lydia is that of rightful authority checked
at every turn by an 'intricate hussy'; and Lydia's tone towards Mrs Malaprop
is that of a heroine imprisoned for love.

The arranged marriage exists in the world today mainly among some
ethnic communities, but the broader issue exists everywhere. Parents and
guardians very often believe that they know what is best for their children,
and children frequently experience the need to challenge this assumption.

4.2 POSING AND PRETENDING

Lydia and Faulkland are both prey to a slight disease of the imagination.
It is a disease for which there is no exact name, though its symptoms are
obvious enough: indulgence in fine feelings for their own sake; the setting
of impossible standards for love and happiness; ignorance and distortion
caused by a romantic image of self. Sentimentality had been reducing
laughter in favour of admiration on the stage for many years, turning
potential comedy into demonstrations of domestic virtue; the sentimental
comedy tended towards a happy outcome moulded by the concept of
poetic justice, where the vicious were punished and the good rewarded. It
is sentimentality of this theatrical variety that renders Faulkland's attitude precious, if not ridiculous:

> If it rains, some shower may even then have chilled her delicate
> frame! If the wind be keen, some rude blast may have affected
> her! The heat of noon, the dews of the evening, may endanger
> the life of her for whom I only value mine.

It is all too good to be true. If it is Faulkland's false concept of the
demands of love that leads him into elaborate poses, it is Lydia's unrealistic
desire to be loved in a certain way that causes her to swing from languor,
to petulance, to ecstasy and back again. Both Faulkland and Lydia have a
set of rules that they apply to the conduct of lovers, and each is mortified
when these rules are broken. From Faulkland's point of view, Julia must
be anti-social, gloomy, pensive and utterly wrapped up in him, whether
he is present or not. As far as Lydia is concerned, Jack can only come up
to her expectations by being poor, often on his knees to her and ready to
encounter any opposition, including ice and snow, on her account. He must
be a hero, but one devoted entirely to pleasing her.

The reason why we are exasperated but at the same time amused by the posturing of Lydia and Faulkland is that it stems from a lack of self-knowledge allied with charming ideals that have more to do with fiction than with life. The pair entirely lack malevolence.

If Lydia and Faulkland mistake their own natures, Bob Acres can be said to impose on himself a nature that doesn't belong to him – he pretends to be what he can never be: a fashionable suitor, but at every turn he is confronted by his real self. He is a master of the *faux pas*, but as for French dances, elegant ladies and polite conversation, where they are concerned, he constantly betrays himself as a product of Clod Hall.

Sir Lucius is a poseur of a more practised kind. His character owes much to the soldier braggart of Roman comedy, and he is unquestionably of the same family as Shakespeare's Pistol (*Henry IV* and *V*). However, Sir Lucius boasts with a difference, which makes him more akin to a character like George Bernard Shaw's La Hire (*St Joan*), in that he means what he says and is not a physical coward. He comes from Blunderbuss Hall, not from Eastcheap like Shakespeare's ranting coward, and he's not only quick to pick a quarrel but as quick to pick a fight. He has posed physically for so long that he is now set into his own image of himself: bluff, swaggering, with a certain old world courtesy at his command. When offended he rears himself up to his full height, puffs out his chest and strides towards his target like an old, faded peacock. He poses because he wishes to give the impression of the aristocrat; he likes to play the part of the wronged hero. He poses because he is arrogant and thinks his friends should hold as great a respect for him as he does for himself. He is Irish, but seems to pose at being most thoroughly Hibernian, now that he is an expatriot. He is, in fact, a stage Irishman, however much Sheridan altered his portrait from the original script, and as a stage Irishman he is himself through and through.

Posing derives largely from the desire to be regarded in a flattering light, and of no one in the play is this more true than of Mrs Malaprop. She would have the world, and in particular Sir Lucius, believe that she is an eligible widow, a social success, sensitive, learned, wise, a mistress of the English language, a great lady of the town. In fact she is none of these, she is a dragon with a soft centre.

Sir Anthony pretends to be a generous and disinterested father, but invariably he acts from a sense that he is in the right and knows what is best for everyone. His play-acting is sporadic and unconvincing, because he only resorts to it when he wishes to put one over on another character.

Putting on airs is by no means confined to the upper stratum of society. Fag poses as a man about town and tries to out-fashion his own master; he is on intimate acquaintance with the servants of all the best households, and speaks with a very superior air; his pretensions are basically snobbish. Lucy is a little villain but wears a 'mask of silliness'. In playing the innocent she supplements her meagre income; so she is something of a professional poseuse.

To what does all this posing and pretending amount? It adds up to Sheridan's portrait of a society that lives too much according to self-interest and to external prescriptions for conduct. The satire is of a gentle kind, not fired by any great reforming zeal; it does not leave a sour taste in the mouth of reader or audience member. Its relevance lies in its laughter at an utterly 'English' and undying range of character and behaviour, and in its close observation of a class that still exists; its main source of comedy is the antics to which certain social conventions drive the characters. What the play is about is, in the final instance, the triumph of true love and common sense (exemplified by Julia and Captain Absolute) over the posturings of vanity and the illusions of selfishness.

5 TECHNICAL FEATURES

5.1 PLOT AND STRUCTURE

spite of its somewhat rambling appearance, the structure of *The Rivals* is as firm as that of most English comedies of this period or of the Restoration. The whole of the action takes place in Bath, and can logically be confined to a single day, although on the stage so much seems to occur that the audience has the sensation of more time passing. The play is allowed to gather its own momentum, however; one episode leads naturally into the next, as Sheridan anticipates the mounting interest of his audience. Although he keeps a firm hand on all strands of the plot, he sometimes over-writes a scene; any director of the play will want to cut some of this over-written material, but this is a difficult task, because stylistically it remains of a high standard. The author has inherited his five-act structure, with its apparent casualness of building scene upon scene, from Congreve, who in his turn learnt it from Shakespeare and Ben Jonson. Without carefully prepared contrasts and parallels, however, the plot would merely sprawl; in fact, its climax and happy outcome can be envisaged long before they arrive. One watches in the course of this play a very gradual disentanglement of simple love from complex snares, so that by the end one is tempted to look back and ask, 'How on earth did they get themselves into such a state in the first place?'

The stories of the two pairs of lovers, which are prefaced by Thomas in the opening scene, run parallel to one another throughout the play and both reach their resolution in the final scene. The intrigue, and the problems, are well explored verbally before Julia and Faulkland meet in III.ii. and before Jack first meets Lydia in III.iii. These two central scenes, central in terms of the span of the play as well as of their importance, present the heart of the matter, and offer contrasting portraits of love distorted. Sheridan knew that to retain the audience's attention he had to make the relationships as different as possible. This he achieved by means of tone as well as of character. After the initial encounters, our main interest is bound to be in how the disorders will be overcome. This focus prevents the play from fragmenting.

Sir Lucius and Acres provide a further elaboration of the main plot, for each regards himself as a suitor to Lydia. Each in his own way impedes a straightforward solution to the crisis and at the same time aggravates it; theirs are highly individual rhythms, the former's heavy and tending towards bombastic slowness, the latter's quick in an oafish way, garrulous and without authority. So each time one of them appears, the play seems to change step as well as tempo. The scenes in which Sir Anthony and Mrs Malaprop appear derive much of their freshness from the irony that we know so much more than they do, and that they suffer from continual misapprehension; this allows the developments of the plot to be diverted in several comic ways.

The Rivals is a long play, and the writing of the second half tends to seem repetitive to a modern audience. Allowing for the fact that Sheridan's contemporaries were more leisurely in their attitude to theatre, there still seem to be imbalances in the structure. The Julia/Faulkland scenes, particularly V.i., need cutting, because otherwise their gravity of style grows excessive and ceases to amuse. Mrs Malaprop is given unnecessarily obvious openings to invent a flush of mistaken words (her discourse on female education being one instance). Jack's reported insult to Sir Lucius does not fit convincingly into the plot, and seems something of an afterthought. In fact, IV.iii.-V.iii. show a slight weakening of creativity on Sheridan's part; that could be accounted for by his practical need to urge all his characters in one direction for the end of the play. Both the urging and the delaying tactics, as in the case of Sir Anthony, become a little obvious. We must not be too heavy in our criticism, though, because Sheridan can never be accused in this play of allowing complications to spoil the development of the action. There are repetitions of effect and the mood is too constant; perhaps there is too much angry confrontation, so that the audience begins to wonder if the comedy has soured; but this makes for variety and allows the last scene to recapture the fullness of the humour. Audiences do need to rest from their laughter.

The final scene is masterly in its unravelling of the plots, even though on the page there may appear to be a certain superficiality in the way that harmony and happiness are induced at the end. Try to understand the difference between the impact that the final pages have on the reader and that produced by the same pages when acted in the theatre. The words themselves may look stilted and conventional, but spoken with conviction they have the sound of joy, and of relief that all the wasteful anxiety is over:

FAULKLAND   Julia! – how can I sue for what I so little deserve? I dare not presume – yet hope is the child of penitence.

JULIA   Oh! Faulkland, you have not been more faulty in your unkind treatment of me, than I am now in wanting inclination to resent it. As my heart honestly bids me place my weakness to the account of love, I should be ungenerous not to admit the same plea for yours.

FAULKLAND   Now I shall be blest indeed!

Julia's rhythmic prose has a heightening effect; suddenly the magic of young and mutual love is in the air. Incidentally, if you will try to rewrite these speeches in modern language, perhaps with a television script in mind, you will discover how hard it is not to be banal, and also how far we have moved from the eighteenth century in terms of emotional expression.

A director of *The Rivals* has to choreograph the final scene almost like a dance, so that some characters are made prominent for a moment – Lucy, for instance – only to disappear almost immediately into the social mêlée behind. If there are loose ends, the general gaiety keeps them from getting tangled.

As in most comedy, the plot and structure of *The Rivals* demonstrate an initial state of confusion that grows worse before becoming gradually clarified; the mess gets sorted out, and bad gets better. The breadth of this play and the depth of its comedy are produced by the author's giving his characters the space and the time to suffer for a love that is improperly returned. Of course, it is not tragic suffering, and we can see the solutions coming. Nevertheless, it is there: without Julia's pain and Jack's frustration, we would have a situation comedy with an accent on the manners of the period; with these elements we have a play where situation, character and manners focus our attention in healthy proportions.

All of the exposition is used practically in the development of the plot, and each major scene in the first three acts has a partner in the last two. The two scenes, III.iv. and IV.i., that take place at Acres' lodgings offer an open road to the climax at King's Mead Fields, once the lovers and their problems have been properly dealt with. The structure ensures that we are not given the time to tire of one situation or one group of characters.

The rapid changes from scene to scene, the varying lengths of the scenes and the change in the number of characters on stage at any one time are all part of a dramatic concept that allows for the broad sweep and the intimate soliloquy, for casual dialogue as well as for the uproar of the thoroughfare.

5.2 CHARACTERISATION

I do not intend to write separate character studies, since these have appeared elsewhere in this book. What does require attention at this point is Sheridan's mode of characterising. Are we to call Mrs Malaprop, Sir Anthony and Bob Acres caricatures, types or fully rounded characters? Can one make a proper distinction between such genres of comic character? What criteria does Sheridan use for creating normal as contrasted with eccentric people?

Restoration comedy, from the plays of George Etherege onwards, developed a gallery of recognisable types: the lawyer, the doctor, the cunning servant, the fop and so on; they were the progeny of mixed dramatic cultures. Roman comedy, Molière, the Elizabethan theory of humours and the unbalanced constitution, Ben Jonson and Shakespeare, could all be found as source material for Restoration comedy characters; add to these the modes and methods of eighteenth-century novel writers and you have the ingredients for a long and fascinating critical game. What concerns us more is the nature of the stage types that Sheridan inherited.

There was the fop, with all his equipage about him, with all his pretensions to wit and fashion evident in the ribbons at his shoulders, as well as in the French adornment of his language. Acres, with his curls and his tailored clothes and his 'sentimental swearing', is a country bumpkin turned out as a fop. Then there was the old curmudgeonly father, looking back at his glorious past and berating his son for not being the man he was. There was the older man besotted with a young girl. There was the conniving servant, male and female; and frequently there was mutton dressed as lamb, an older lady believing herself loved or lovable by a much younger man, and making a great deal of fuss about the tender emotions. There was the lady who wanted to be thought intellectually superior and there was the stage cavalier; there were the vain beauty and the hoyden.

Many of Sheridan's characters bear traces of one or more of these. Can you identify them? Any good playwright, however, who uses types, adds to their dimension from his experience of people. Sheridan knows his eccentrics from the inside, as well as from the outside, just as Rowlandson, the great cartoonist of the period, knew his; the dramatist and cartoonist have to live inside their creations to prevent them from becoming mere surfaces. In confining his vision to their salient features, Sheridan does not stoop to cheap caricature; these types are living flesh and blood, not abstracts. This is partly a result of the exuberance of Sheridan's imagination. Mrs Malaprop derives her linguistic contortions from Shakespeare's Dogberry (*Much Ado About Nothing*), and Bottom (*A Midsummer Night's Dream*) as well as from a character in one of Sheridan's mother's plays, and yet they seem utterly her own, because the author has lavished on her so many beautiful errors that are highly individual and completely consistent with her mental set, to use a current phrase. Can you imagine any other character saying, 'She's as headstrong as an allegory on the banks of Nile' or 'He is the very pineapple of politeness'? She is a definite type, easily recognised, yet absolutely unique. And doesn't that correspond with a great many people in life – at least, until you know them well?

Most of the others are in the same vein. Sir Anthony differs from his literary predecessors by the gout that seems to have attacked his brain, and by the purely matter-of-fact way in which he regards his son as a possession, to be disposed of as he deems fit. Bob Acres is rustic and fop rolled into one. Sir Lucius is the conventional braggart, but he turns out to have courage to the point of recklessness. The peculiarites of Faulkland's and Lydia's dispositions are inherited from the more recent sentimental comedy, as we have previously said. All the time, we can detect Sheridan regarding a traditional type through the prism of his own sense of humour and so producing a highly individual version of that type.

There remain Julia and Capt. Absolute. It does little good for a reader, or for an actor or director, to address himself to Julia's character with the psychological assumption that for her to cling to Faulkland in spite of all his cruelty is tantamount to masochism. As with Geoffrey Chaucer and his patient Griselde (*The Clerk's Tale*), Sheridan's focus is largely on the sweetness and perseverance in his heroine's nature, rather than on some negative aspect of her relationship with the man she loves. Her patient sacrifice is in contrast to Lydia's caprice, and it is an aesthetic as well as a moral contrast. Similarly, Capt. Absolute's eager pursuit of his beloved contrasts with Faulkland's spying out of Julia's supposed faults. Julia and Capt. Absolute have a parentage in common-sense heroes, in Shakespeare's Viola (*Twelfth Night*) or Aimwell (George Farquhar's *The Beaux' Stratagem*), but their robustness, their humour and their inability to pose and attitudinise mark them out as creatures of Sheridan's mind. Their ability to endure leads them to the edge of both farce and tragedy, but at each stage they become more resolutely themselves.

In most plays character is defined by means of contrast, but in *The Rivals* this is particularly clear to see. Each character is paired with another, not just in terms of age or status or family relationship, but rather by similarity and opposition, so that both characters are highlighted and enriched. Obviously, Mrs Malaprop has a family relationship to Lydia, as does Sir Anthony to Jack; but it is the combination of the aunt and the father that is the true and theatrical relationship. The blunderbuss is paired with 'fighting Bob', the manipulating Lucy is set off by the superior-minded Fag. Without the scenes between these couples, we should not get to know their real qualities or learn to enjoy their limitations so much. Bob's cowardice becomes a joke when it is matched with Sir Lucius's demands for honour, and Fag and Lucy seem most themselves when they are trying to steal the last laugh off one another at the end of II.ii.

The lovers are paired twice. Take Faulkland. Obviously he is paired and contrasted with Julia. She is generous where he is jealous, she is resolute whereas he wavers, she trusts and he doesn't. Her sweetness and light make him seem at moments sour and dark; in the first scene they have together Sheridan has given Julia a joyful entrance, full of her love for Faulkland. It is this that makes his prudery extreme, comic and painful to listen to, all at the same time:

> Well then – shall I own to you that my joy at hearing of your health and arrival here, by your neighbour Acres, was somewhat damped, by his dwelling much on the high spirits you had enjoyed in Devonshire – on your mirth – your singing – dancing, and I know not what! For such is my temper, Julia, that I should regard every mirthful moment in your absence as a treason to constancy: the mutual tear that steals down the cheek of parting lovers is a compact, that no smile shall live there till they meet again.

Imagine what kind of a scene we should have if Julia suffered from the same kind of temperament as Faulkland.

But Faulkland is also paired with Jack. They are opposites in some aspects of their behaviour, and yet one can see why they are friends. They complement one another; Jack's straightforwardness is made more pronounced by Faulkland's tortuousness, and vice versa. Similarly, Lydia is matched with Jack and paired with Julia. Her languishing nature contrasts with her lover's but also with her friend's. What all the lovers share in common is love itself, which none of the other characters seem capable of understanding; for them there are few ideals attached to the prospect of marriage. This hope of a happiness not yet enjoyed is one way in which the lovers are contrasted as a group with everyone else. The effect should be seen not only in their passions, but in the cut and colour of their clothes; it should be in the energy of their movement and in the tone of their voices. Character and colour go together; Jack Absolute is as bright as his red coat. So what colours should Lydia and Faulkland wear?

5.3 STYLE AND LANGUAGE

The language or conventions of dialogue that a dramatist employs need to be analysed from two angles. From the first point of view we observe general features of style. Shakespeare used blank verse, rhyming couplets, and rhythmic prose, and achieved the greatest possible variety with each. The subtext in a play of Henrik Ibsen or Anton Chekhov (all those emotions and thoughts that lie between the lines but are not stated in them) is as essential to it as the words themselves. In *Waiting for Godot* the business that Samuel Beckett has devised for the tramps and for Lucky and Pozzo is as important as the verbal language. So what are the distinctive features of Sheridan's dramatic medium? For him, as for the rest of the play-wrights of his age, stage business was rarely independent of the dialogue. If props were to be used, they were made prominent. Letters, money passed from hand to hand, Beverley's miniature, Lydia's books: when these appear, they become the subject of the conversation. When a director gives an actor incidental business to perform in a play of this kind, he has to be very careful that the point of the scene does not get lost. For instance, it might be tempting to have Mrs Malaprop and Capt. Absolute take tea together in III.iii., but how easily the timing can be spoilt by the clatter of china. The focus is not primarily physical. We can say as much about the whole play.

Where the dialogue allows it, Sheridan writes finished prose. His sentences are often pleasing to listen to for their logical construction and rounded cadence, even if the speaker himself lacks logic. Bob Acres's explanation of 'sentimental swearing' in I.ii. is a good example. This is not spoken thought but written language. It is fluently expressed, and the spontaneity lies in the choice of words and the feeling behind them; Sheridan does not make Bob inarticulate as a modern dramatist might choose to do. The fool in a Comedy of Manners usually hangs himself with his own words; his greatest pride is his greatest folly and in speaking of that, he renders himself ridiculous. When we think we see the virtues and vices of these characters, it is usually because we hear about them first. Verbal jokes of every kind set in a context of polite and sometimes elevated prose: these are the hallmark of Sheridan's age in a world that thrived on conversation, and they are the secret of Sheridan's style – the slight pomposity and the puncturing phrase; the beautifully turned speech that goes nowhere; the language is a superb vehicle for self-betrayal. Here we come to our second point of view.

Character manifests itself not only in the content of a speech but in the choice of words, that is, the diction, in the length of each sentence and the way in which the sentences are built up, in syntax and in punctuation, in italicised phrases and in the contrast between the rhythm of one line and that of the next:

ABSOLUTE   Oh, come to me - rich only thus - in loveliness - bring no portion to me but thy love - 'twill be generous in you, Lydia - for well you know, it is the only dower your poor Beverley can repay.

LYDIA   How persuasive are his words! How charming will poverty be with him!

We hear Absolute improvising for his life through those romantic dashes, and we hear Lydia yielding to his imagery in her equally romantic exclamation marks! Her combination of the words 'charming' and 'poverty' leaves us in no doubt as to the unrealistic aspect of her dreams. Absolute's absurdly sentimental speech that follows lends itself to the puncturing technique; his aside is as blunt as can be after all the hyperboles: 'If she holds out now the devil is in it!'

It should have become clear by now that each character has a particular vocabulary, and a particular way of stringing words together. These add up to a verbal personality. Where appropriate, dialect is used to highlight this. Acres is full of Clod Hall phrases, though too marked a country accent would be wrong as it would remove him entirely from Jack's social sphere; Sir Lucius is resonantly Irish; Lucy may come from the West Country; Fag may occasionally fall into cockney when he is agitated. Sheridan has the detachment necessary to a writer of high comedy, with the result that part of our enjoyment is gained from distinguishing between the language and style of a role and the tone the playwright adopts towards that role. A kind of ideal hovers around the language of the play, and we witness folly and vanity in the light of it. The name Malaprop is derived from the French phrase *mal à propos*, meaning inappropriate. Sheridan gives his actress a definite stage direction when he has Julia describe her: 'with her select words so ingeniously *misapplied* without being *mispronounced*'. It is most important that she should preserve the correct pronunciation of the words; if she goes wrong in two directions at once, we shall not know what to laugh at. Anyway, her external fastidiousness about such things is part of what makes her amusing. Usually the words that she misapplies do not need searching for: they are on the tip of her tongue; they are the wrong words but they sound like what she means; we as an audience enjoy a feeling of recognition each time we hear her go wrong. We have all misused words and blushed to remember our misuse. The great thing about the malapropisms in this play is that they go entirely unchecked and their perpetrator remains blissfully ignorant of the laughter she provokes.

Although the words she selects are often funny in the context, that cannot account for the laughter with which they are greeted. The audience reaction usually follows the reaction of the character whom Mrs Malaprop is addressing. For instance, in Mrs Malaprop's long speech about female education we take our cues from Sir Anthony as he registers surprise, amusement and delight at the torrent of misapplied words.

There are times when she hits upon a word that seems to have no obvious parallel in the world of sense. What does she really mean when she calls Lydia an 'intricate hussy'? And what is her thought behind the choice of 'simony' as one of the subjects she would have a young woman avoid? The answer on these occasions seems to be that the word itself is ridiculous enough under the circumstances not to need a direct parallel. It was astute of Sheridan to leave the audience floundering occasionally in search of Mrs Malaprop's intended meaning; he was, after all, writing a play, not a crossword puzzle.

5.4 STAGECRAFT

The scenes
Variety of scene is one of the greatest merits of *The Rivals*; it is largely achieved by interspersing interior scenes with exteriors. Contrast in mood, setting and action is always vivid. The length of scene is expertly judged, except perhaps in the case of V. i.

Dialogue
The best thing about the dialogue is that it is so unforced; Sheridan's young mind was teeming with ideas, and he seems to have known well enough what his actors could handle, which lines could be delivered and how they had to be shaped. His rhythms help his actors, and his punctuation is a surer guide to comic delivery than any stage directions would be. His distribution of dialogue and his use of the occasional silence for a character are difficult to fault. When long speeches occur, they arise directly out of the situation, and focus the audience's attention not just on the speaker's frame of mind but on what is going to happen. Soliloquys and asides engage the audience as partners to the speaker, without necessarily implying agreement with his or her sentiments. Sheridan is a master of the aside, and uses it to the best effect in the tightest situations.

Exits and entrances
These are planned in a natural way that allows for a rapid change of pace, volume and energy for the next unit. You will see this in Acres' entrance in II.i., where he bursts into the quiet conversation concerning him as though he has been thrown from his horse straight into Jack's

room. The entering or exiting actor is always given preferential treatment.

Stage directions
These are the directions of a writer used to the practicalities of the stage. 'Bursts into tears', 'Flings herself into a chair, with her face from the door', 'Puts himself in an "attitude"' these are clear, physical directions person must have their 'moment': this applies to the actor as well as to the possible. Some of the stage directions may have been taken from the action as it developed on stage; the majority Sheridan would have written before he handed the script to the manager. We know that it was written in haste, and this might account for the uneven distribution of stage directions.

Giving the actor the stage
In a play like this, where character is of paramount importance, each person must have their 'moment': this applies to the actor as well as to role. Sheridan, either through instinct or the experience that he disclaimed, knew how to bring one character after another into prominence. Consider how easily he could have let Lucy go at the end of I.ii. without allowing her time to reveal her true nature. But if he had, she would have failed to capture our special interest early in the play. Fag's laboured precision in V.i. suddenly throws a new light upon him at the moment when he seems to be forgotten. Each actor gets his break, yet at some moment each is little more than a foil to his or her fellow.

Asides and soliloquies
These build up an intimate relationship between the actor and the audience. Sheridan is careful not to disrupt the action when he uses them: that is what happens in pantomime. The soliloquy here is not a reflective medium, it informs us directly about the character of the speaker or about the situation; it is usually accompanied by some physical action that makes the speech something of a 'turn'. The aside is usually spoken straight out to the audience, though not directed to any particular member of it.

Letters
How many letters or written messages are there in the play? What do they contribute to the plot? Remember, there was no telephone and no typewriter. The handwritten letter or note is a very common means of advancing a plot in plays written before the twentieth century. The Greeks used a messenger; we use the 'phone. Sheridan makes the best use of a letter as a dramatic device in III.iii. where it is a visible reminder of the scene's irony; there Jack sits, coolly reading out his own insults to Mrs Malaprop,

while she scoffs at the very idea of Beverley getting through her net: ' - elude my vigilance! Yes, yes, ha! ha! ha!' We watch the letter itself as if it were a captured flag.

Comedy technique

Sheridan knew instinctively, and no doubt as a result of his early training, both how to invite laughter from an audience and how to build small laughs towards a big one. He was a true professional, and you will find very little wasted or ill-timed comedy in this play. Rhythm is the key to much of it, and Sheridan is particularly adept at contrasting rhythms in the dialogue:

SIR LUCIUS   Why, you may think there's no being shot at without a little risk - and if an unlucky bullet should carry a *quietus* with it - I say it will be no time then bothering you about family matters.

ACRES   A *quietus*!

SIR LUCIUS   For instance now - if that should be the case - would you choose to be pickled and sent home? or would it be the same to you to lie here in the Abbey? I'm told there is very snug lying in the Abbey.

ACRES   Pickled! Snug lying in the Abbey! Odds tremors! Sir Lucius, don't talk so!

SIR LUCIUS   I suppose, Mr Acres, you never were engaged in an affair of this kind before?

Sir Lucius is slow and easy, positively bland in his questioning; Acres, terrified at the prospect of his approaching end, can only jabber and repeat. The laughs that actors can elicit in this passage are numerous, but they have to remember that there are louder ones to come; Acres' 'Clean through me! - a ball or two clean through me!' can be what actors call 'a show-stopper'. All this would be of little relevance, if Sheridan himself had not catered to the actors' needs.

Although verbal comedy has been stressed throughout this guide as being of prime importance, it is evident that the play contains a good deal of physical comedy as well. This too shows what a thorough understanding of the stage Sheridan had. Mrs Malaprop's concealment in III.iii. would have been easier to execute in eighteenth-century scenery than it is today, but even now it can be one of the comic highlights of a production. Notice that Sheridan is careful to keep the whole episode brief; if extended it could very well destroy the audience's willing suspension of disbelief. The actors are left to discover for themselves the large amount of physical business required by IV.ii. for there is no way in which

Sheridan could have given stage directions to cover it; anyway, he liked to make his actors work. Such incidents as Acres' dance practice and the beginning of the duel scene rely on strong, visual comedy to support the words, and vice versa.

As with all the finest writers of comedy, Sheridan has consciously, or unconsciously, concealed funny moments, which are only revealed during a performance. I find this to be true of several scenes in which Faulkland appears. On the page, his excesses can become boring, while on the stage they can be made increasingly enjoyable.

6 SPECIMEN PASSAGE AND COMMENTARY

There are a few rules for analysing dramatic text which I think it would be worthwhile stating before we look at a selected passage. Like all rules, they are made to be broken on specific occasions, but they provide a basic approach.

1. State the context of the passage briefly and clearly; otherwise you will find yourself having to refer back to it in a most clumsy manner.
2. Remember that this is a play, not a novel or a film. The stage has its particular methods of presentation, as well as its limitations.
3. The reason for things being said is as important as what is said.
4. A speech represents a sequence of thoughts, not one big thought that comes at the beginning.
5. Scenes change direction.
6. Try to keep the author in mind; he chose specific words, as a poet does, to create desired effects. Assume that nothing in the text arrived there by chance, and that, therefore, all of it has a purpose. If at first it seems obscure, look again, and keep your mind's eye fixed on the stage.
7. It is a game to be played, using the tools of observation and deduction. You have to observe character, language and action, in order to decide how the dramatist has shaped the scene. Textual analysis is not a form to be filled in, but a critical activity that is at the heart of the scholar's, the actor's and the director's work. It is not something that has been fabricated to make English or drama classes hard work. Indeed, it should be fun.

The passage that follows has been chosen for several reasons. It is short and reasonably self-contained. It is typical in some ways and unusual in others. The advantage of using this exchange between David and Acres is that, although it is less complicated than a passage from one of the major scenes, it will, I hope, give scope for a clear method of analysis to be shown.

Acres' lodgings.
Acres as just dressed and David.

ACRES   Indeed, David – do you think I become it so?

DAVID   You are quite another creature, believe me Master, by the mass! An' we've any luck we shall see the Devon monkeyrony in all the print-shops in Bath!

ACRES   Dress *does* make a difference, David.

DAVID   'Tis all in all, I think – difference! Why, an' you were to go now to Clod Hall, I am certain the old lady wouldn't know you: Master Butler wouldn't believe his own eyes, and Mrs Pickle would cry, 'Lard presarve me!'. Our dairy-maid would come giggling to the door, and I warrant Dolly Tester, your honour's favourite, would blush like my waistcoat. Oons! I'll hold a gallon, there an't a dog in the house but would bark, and I question whether Phillis would wag a hair of her tail!

ACRES   Aye, David, there's nothing like *polishing*.

DAVID   So I says of your honour's boots; but the boy never heeds me!

ACRES   But, David, has Mr De-la-Grace been here? I must rub up my balancing, and chasing, and boring.

DAVID   I'll call again, Sir.

ACRES   Do – and see if there are any letters for me at the post-office.

DAVID   I will. – By the mass, I can't help looking at your head! If I hadn't been by at the cooking, I wish I may die if I should have known the dish again myself.   *Exit.*

Acres comes forward, practising a dancing step.

ACRES   Sink, slide – coupee – confound the first inventors of cotillons! say I – they are as bad as algebra to us country gentlemen – I can walk a minuet easily enough when I'm forced! – and I have been accounted a good stick in a country dance. Odds jigs and tabors! I never valued your cross over to couple – figure in – right and left – and I'd foot it with e'er a captain in the county! – but these out-landish heathen allemandes and cotillons are quite beyond me! – I shall never prosper at 'em, that's sure – mine are true-born English legs – they don't understand their cursed French lingo! – their *pas* this, and *pas* that, and *pas* t'other! – damn me, my feet don't like to be called paws! No, 'tis certain I have most antigallican toes! (III.iv)

Commentary

Bob Acres has been sent to Bath by his mother, whom he has referred to earlier in the play as 'ancient Madam'. However, he is happy with the match she has arranged for him, and is determined to woo Lydia Languish in the style befitting a gentleman. He has trained his hair into the latest curled fashion and got rid of his old leather breeches and hunting frock. The outfit he has donned for the present scene, and in which he will most likely remain for the rest of the play, makes him look like a gilded ass. What colour do you think he is wearing? Is it perhaps a little too bright? The coat is cut away, the shoulders broad; the trousers are too tight and accentuate his Clod Hall gait. David is wearing some kind of livery in which he is not altogether comfortable. Acres is obviously set to impress the town.

Acres begins the scene with a response to something that David has said off-stage. We can infer from the words ' . . . do you think I become it so?' that David has been flattering his master's attire. Acres fishes for compliments in a tone of pleased surprise, and his servant apparently supplies them; but 'quite another creature' corresponds in tone to the American expression 'something else', and can be ambiguous, depending on how it is said. Certainly Acres has changed, but whether for the better or not is a matter of taste. David's expostulation, 'by the mass!' registers a certain degree of amazement at the transformation. Though his tone is flattering, the expressions he chooses are not altogether so. A 'Devon monkeyrony' is almost a contradiction in terms, for a successful fop is as unlikely to come from that part of the world as a cowherd from within the sound of Bow Bells. The print-shops to which David alludes exhibited portraits of celebrities; imagine the face of Acres smiling out of a shop window between those of David Garrick and James Boswell. With studied nonchalance Acres accepts the compliment as utterly deserved: 'Dress does make a difference, David.' This is a cue for enthusiasm, and David rises to it; but his enthusiasm has a sting in its tail. Let us look carefully at the speech Sheridan has written for David, to make sure that we don't misinterpret it. Acres hears nothing beyond a servant's congratulations; we hear an ambiguity in the words that makes us think they should not be taken at face value. The reactions of Master Butler, Mrs Pickle and the rest could be induced by the preposterous as well as by the splendid, while the barking of dogs and the failure of Phillis to wag her tail are the reactions that we might associate with an animal that has just seen a ghost rather than its returning master!

There are several items of vocabulary in this speech that need to be noted. The names of the servants categorise them, and in the case of Mrs Pickle her name suggests the type of woman she is; her dialect, as indicated by the phonetic spelling of 'Lard presarve' may be overlaid with a slightly genteel accent. A tester is the canopy that stands above a bed, which implies that Dolly Tester is a chambermaid. Since she is Bob Acres' favourite, according to David, it seems fair to infer in passing that Sheridan wishes us to perceive that Acres is more at home with the maids than with fine ladies like Lydia Languish. If Dolly Tester's blush would resemble the colour of David's waistcoat, then at least that part of his livery must be red. 'Oons' is a West Country form of 'zounds', one of the commonest expletives of the period, which by this time had completely lost its religious significance, as had David's favourite invocation, 'by the mass!'. When he says that he'll 'hold a gallon', he means that he's ready to bet a gallon of ale.

Acres misses the innuendo in all this, and asserts that there is nothing like *polishing*. By this he means making himself smart, and fit for society. In applying the word literally to his master's boots, David makes Acres seem pretentious, though in this case it's doubtful whether his joke is conscious. 'The boy never heeds me' – Acres' boots are always a mess: this is the sort of hint that a costume designer has to work from.

Until now we have had one unit of the scene. The topic of conversation now changes, as does the tempo. Acres is even more concerned with learning his dance steps than with parading his clothes. *The Rivals* is written and set in the age of the dancing master. Any gentleman intent on entering society must be able to dance, particularly the latest French steps. Unfortunately for the image he is trying to create, when he talks of balancing, chasing and boring, which describe elegant movements in dancing, Bob sounds as though he is speaking of blood sports. An actor can have a lovely time mouthing these words with a knowing air. One can imagine that Mr De-la-Grace (of Gracefulness) does not look forward to his visits here. There is an implication that he has not turned up recently.

An actor has to decide what to do with every line; unless he interprets fully, he cannot be content. How is David to say that short line, 'I'll call again, Sir'? It can be taken purely at face value: a servant's stock response. Does he start to leave, to call on the dancing master? Then again, it could be that David is just standing there, watching his master, and trying to conceal the laughter that keeps bubbling up inside him. Do we see him smile? Perhaps – and this might be a director's touch – David straightens Acres' coat or brushes fluff from a lapel in order to hide his mirth. 'Do' – Acres dismisses his servant with a waft of the hand, like an emperor. The letters at the post-office are an afterthought; it is as though Acres, great man that he now is according to his own lights, believes there should be a bundle of mail waiting for him. David is about to leave when he once more catches sight of his master's curled pate; this time he seems to laugh openly; he is still incredulous at the sight, even though he had watched the hair being heated and rolled like a dish being cooked. This is the nearest David comes to being rude. How does Acres take it? Does he again take it as a compliment, or has he stopped concentrating in order to start practising his dance steps? Either way, David's exit ends the second unit of the scene.

Acres' speech is more like a virtuoso comic turn than a soliloquy. He moves downstage, closer to the audience, practising his moves, 'Sink, slide - coupee -'. He suits the action to the word, bending his knees and then stepping to the right: a movement that should be graceful but which he executes very awkwardly. Notice that there is only a comma between the first two words, and a dash between 'slide' and 'coupee'; the latter punctuation may be a pause while Acres summons up the courage to launch himself into what is supposed to be a bow. Presumably he is not pleased with his results, and indeed it is possible that he nearly falls over, for he curses the inventors of the dance hs is trying to learn: the cotillon. This was one of the few dances Faulkland regarded as legitimate for Julia to participate in: a polite and graceful thing quite outside Bob's rustic talents. By aligning cotillons with algebra Acres brands them as nonsense. His ordinary dancing isn't so bad, he claims, and his country dancing has been praised, 'a good stick in a country dance' - what a perfectly chosen phrase! It is Bob in a nutshell. He suddenly seems to warm to his subject; the actor needs to be fired with a real dislike of the task the dancing master has given him. He is like a spoilt child in the corner, kicking the floor and saying 'I won't! I can't!' 'Odds jigs and tabors' is a 'sentimental oath'. He says he never worried about the movements required in a country dance, and that he'd be ready to compete in one of those with any captain in Devon, but as for the German and French dances, with all their strange contortions - these are heathen things and right outside his range. The choice of the word 'heathen' is excellent; it catches Acres' fear as well as his distaste.

Acres acknowledges crossly that he'll never succeed at these dances, which means he already foresees that he's doomed to be an outsider in Bath. He stands there, in all his fancy dress, a slightly sad figure for a moment, the victim of his own illusions. Then he decides to justify his failure: his legs are English legs, so no wonder they can't be taught to dance in the French language. The pun between *pas* and 'paws' is beautifully timed to invite the audience's laughter; this can be encouraged by Acres looking down at his farmer's feet in their courtier's shoes. The final line, which is meant to pave the way for the entrance of Sir Lucius, has to be said proudly and patriotically if it is to make sense. His toes are 'antigallican' because they are the enemies of France, the traditional foe of England; the cotillon was a symbol of French corruption, and therefore it was a good thing not to be able to dance it!

7 IN REHEARSAL

This chapter is a way of concentrating on one aspect of textual analysis: the physicalisation process that has to take place in the imagination of the reader. It can hardly be repeated too often that a play is not a novel in dialogue form, and that it is a critical error to forget about the stage for which it was intended. *The Rivals* is most definitely a score for performance. Only an expert group of actors can bring all the comic moments to light while allowing the themes to register sufficiently strongly.

Imagine you are attending a rehearsal for III.iii., starting at Mrs Malaprop's entrance. We are in Mrs Malaprop's lodgings; the designer intends the room to look rich but pretentious and a little blown out of proportion like its owner. This he has achieved with a few bold measures. The theatre cannot accommodate grooves and shutters; instead we have a series of drapes and pictures that are flown in, and scenic units that are pushed in from the wings. These items maintain the unconcealed theatricality of eighteenth-century theatre but create an atmosphere. The location is easily recognised from the presence of two outsize chandeliers adorned with a cluster of ribbons, like Mrs Malaprop herself. There is a pair of painted Chinese screens on either side of the room, on which she-dragons are in evidence. Above the one that stands stage right (left as the audience sees it) hangs a large portrait of a florid gentleman, Mrs Malaprop's husband, now deceased. Downstage of the stage left screen is an elaborate, gilt-framed mirror, encircled with flowers and cherubs; this is a frequent stopping place for both Lydia and Mrs Malaprop. In the centre of the stage are a delicate settee and two very upright chairs to match; the upholstery on them is cream and cherry-coloured and has a busy floral pattern which the discerning spectator will see duplicated with a slight difference on Mrs Malaprop's afternoon gown, as she enters from the stairs which can just be seen obtruding from behind the upstage left screen. The stage direction is 'Enter Mrs Malaprop, *listening*'. The actress must be seen to be listening. 'Mrs Malaprop is a little deaf', the director tells the actress concerned, 'particularly in her left ear! And you are coming on too early; if you don't allow Lydia to finish her line about coming to a crisis, you don't allow her to finish that unit with a pose, which she must do if our attention is not going to be divided.'

'Yes, I see that,' says the actress playing Mrs Malaprop, 'but my first line, 'I'm impatient to know how the little hussy deports herself' takes an age to deliver as I traipse down the stairs. Can I come on quickly and say this loud and clear in the direction of the audience, from the bottom of the stairs?'

'Try it', says the director – his most frequent exhortation. She does so, and some actors who are sitting around laugh at her eager manner. On tiptoes but without much agility she advances a few feet and takes refuge behind the stage-left screen. As soon as she arrives, she thrusts her head out and in strangled tones repeats Absolute's words, 'warmth abated!'

'Those words are in italics in the text. Misunderstand Absolute more completely. Each time you have finished your line, duck back behind the screen for fear that he is going to turn upstage and see you.'

Lydia says 'Think not the idle threats of my ridiculous aunt can ever have any weight with me.' There has been some trouble with this moment because the young actress playing Lydia insisted on emphasising the 'ridiculous aunt' which made it sound as though she knew she was there. Now she has the proper balance of the sentence, and when Mrs Malaprop emerges, somewhat more slowly, from behind the screen, the effect is funny. 'Very dutiful, upon my word!' expostulates Mrs Malaprop with much chin wagging; then, picking up the screen without folding it, she moves about three feet closer to them; as she parks again, Absolute thinks he hears something, but decides he is mistaken. The actors must be careful not to descend to cheap pantomime. Mrs Malaprop can be relied on to provide the laughs. As she waddles forward, her feet just visible beneath the screen, the effect is of a brightly painted tank that changes direction silently.

In spite of the fact that Lydia's line, 'Let her choice be Captain Absolute, but Beverley is mine.' is said in tones of idealistic rapture, Mrs Malaprop continues to misinterpret the duet completely. Her head pops out from the other side of the screen this time, as though she is surveying the territory from all sides like a sniper. After 'this to his face!', she ducks behind again, picks up the screen and advances – just a foot, because Jack's sudden act of kneeling and his passionate appeal bring her to a halt. She peers round the screen, aghast to see her hero in such a forlorn state.

'Don't just emerge, Mrs Malaprop; reveal yourself, as Sheridan requests

- in the full flourish of your righteous indignation. Good, that's better.' She seems to expand with hot air as she appears, then to charge rather than walk on 'Why thou vixen! - I have overheard you.'

First, Absolute's line, his aside, 'Oh, confound her vigilance!' is delivered from the kneeling position; this does not work because it leaves the women with nothing to do. 'Get up and move away from both of them as you say the line in a half-whisper to the audience', the director suggests. The actor does this well enough, but doesn't seem to know why he is making the move. 'You feel, however irrationally, that the further away you are, the less likely either of them is to discover your hoax. Try rubbing your knee as you get up, it will make the action more prosaic.' Mrs Malaprop is not one to be shaken off. All decorum and fluster, having swallowed her dragon's flames for a moment, she pursues him with apologies on Lydia's behalf. 'You need to address them as though they are the good and the bad angel. When you say 'Captain Absolute' it should sound as though you are offering him Turkish delight. Absolute's, 'So - all's safe, I find.' does not sound like an aside; ever since rehearsals began, the actor has had difficulty mastering the art of the aside. The director tells him that it must be an intimate declaration as though to a single member of the audience; by contrast 'I have hopes, Madam, that time will bring the young lady —' should sound formal, even public.

Now that the triangle of confusion is firmly established, there's hardly any need for movement until near the end of the exchange. 'She's as headstrong as an allegory on the banks of Nile' does not fail to raise a laugh, even from watching actors. It is worth stating the obvious: Mrs Malaprop must never seem to know that she has used the wrong word; there is a fine balance between hammering a word and relishing it. At this point Mrs Malaprop stands between the two lovers, firing questions and exclamations at her niece, berating her for her ill manners, and turning every few lines to her good angel, beseeching his pardon with fan and hand and bend of head, and then again turning on Lydia with increased venom.

The lovers exchange glances behind the old lady's back, and on Lydia's, "Tis true, Ma'am, and none but Beverley —' she blows him a kiss; as Mrs Malaprop, outraged at her boldness, rounds on her, Absolute, with a romantic sigh that seems to thrill through his whole body, blows the kiss back with a gesture of recklessness. If the laughs are for the most part at the expense of the aunt, the last one is in irony at the niece: 'May every blessing wait on my Beverley.'

The exit is intentionally messy: 'But come with me, Miss —' is literal enough. Mrs Malaprop grabs Lydia's arm and proceeds to draw her upstage left towards the stairs. 'With the force of your move, swing Lydia round in the direction of Absolute. Jack, seize Lydia's hand; squeeze it tenderly.

Lydia, cry out, but lose hold; stretch out towards your beloved Ensign; gaze at each other. Good.' When the 'graceful leave' that Mrs Malaprop commands turns out to be further rudeness, as she thinks – the mere name of Beverley is rudeness under such circumstances – she smothers Lydia's final words with her hands. Jack blows Lydia a series of kisses and signals reassuringly behind Mrs Malaprop's back, and when the old lady turns, it is to smile kindly at the young Captain to whom she has taken such a fancy, after which, with a swift tug at Lydia, she leaves. Jack sighs, recollects the problems that await him, and – 'Stride courageously into the future, Jack', the director calls. The harpsichord plays a stately piece by Thomas Arne, the major English composer of the period, as the scene is changed to Acres' lodgings.

8 CRITICAL RECEPTION

Probably the harshest criticism *The Rivals* has ever received came after its disastrous first night. The *Morning Post*, 21 January 1775, had this to say about the most controversial aspect of the play: 'This representation of Sir Lucius, is indeed an affront to the common sense of an audience, and is so far from giving the manners of our brave and worthy neighbours, that it scarce equals the picture of a respectable Hottentot.' After some revision and a reassignment of the role, Sir Lucius O'Trigger became not only acceptable but an audience favourite, a stock Irish gentleman but at that level unsurpassed.

Dr Samuel Johnson, the great writer and critic, called *The Rivals* and *The Duenna* 'the two best comedies of the age'. We would not be inclined to bracket the play and the operetta together, but that may be because we are seldom treated to a production of *The Duenna*. The praise is high, but no one seems to have argued strongly against it until after *The School for Scandal* had overshadowed the earlier comedies.

Fifty years after the first production, in 1825, Thomas Moore, Sheridan's biographer, wrote that in *The Rivals* Sheridan 'overcharged most of his persons with whims and absurdities, for which the circumstances they are engaged in afford but a very disproportionate vent'. In other words, Moore found the play full of eccentric caricatures who have nothing to do except show how eccentric they are. Certainly there is a tendency to burlesque in the piece that can't be denied when it is compared with *The School for Scandal*. The play suffered something of a critical eclipse because of this kind of evaluation, but it did not cease to be performed in the theatre.

There would be no sense in trying to claim for *The Rivals* qualities that it lacks. To dismiss it as slight or merely boisterous, however, as critics have occasionally done, would be to ignore both the emotional build-up of the play to its happy *dénouement* and the contradictory reactions among critics and audiences to Sheridan's use of sentimental comedy in various scenes. Faulkland has always been at the centre of this controversy.

The *Morning Chronicle*, 27 January 1775, contained this eulogy: 'Faulkland is a great proof of heart-felt delicacy; he is a beautiful exotic, and tho' not found in every garden, we cannot deny it may in some; the exquisite refinement in his disposition, opposed to the noble simplicity, tenderness, and candor of Julia's, gives rise to some of the most affecting sentimental scenes I ever remember to have met with.' Few of us would agree with this assessment of Faulkland's character, and I do not believe it was the impact Sheridan intended. Nevertheless, there is more than a grain of truth in it, and it is that which can lead to discomfort for the reader or audience. Sheridan had a degree of sympathy for the sentimental, and for the exquisite fantasy of Lydia as well as for the self-afflicted jealousy of Faulkland. We tend to tire of him too soon, because he is too serious, too self-centred and too wordy. A generation more given to enjoying manners for their own sake might find Jack just a little too healthy and outgoing for their taste. I have frequently heard the observation made that Faulkland is a fool and consequently boring. Far from being a fool, he is an intellectual whose blinkers are constantly in danger of being removed. But it is no good countering such character assassination with references to social behaviour in the eighteenth century or to literary precedence. The final test of success must be on the stage, and there the whole sentimental side of the play, satirical or not, does pose a critical problem.

In *Sheridan and the Drama of Georgian England* John Loftis carries out a thorough investigation of *The Rivals* and *The Duenna*. As a modern critic he shares with many contemporaries the view that *The Rivals* is conventional and derivative, but that this enhances its entertainment value. He sees the satire as being thoroughly diluted by the charm of character. Although he regards authorial haste as being to blame for an excess of situational humour, nevertheless he categorises the comedy as one of character:

> The play is not without a strong narrative line. Misrepresentations and misunderstandings follow hard on one another. Yet the narrative functions primarily as a means of displaying the absurdities of the characters. The barriers confronting the two couples are of their own making, deriving either from over-active imaginations or from ignorance of their tyrannical elders' intentions.

This seems to me to get the priorities right, always remembering that character is not only individual, but an expression of some portion of the age's manners.

REVISION QUESTIONS

1. What are the major themes in *The Rivals*, and how are they expressed in the action of the play?

2. Lydia Languish is told by her aunt that 'thought does not become a young woman'; Sir Anthony laments the 'natural consequence of teaching girls to read'. Discuss these sentiments in the light of the play as a whole. How would they be regarded in today's society?

3. What does either Bob Acres *or* Sir Lucius O'Trigger contribute to the plot?

4. The major characters in *The Rivals* are paired with one another. Choose *one* of the following pairs and explain their similarities and differences:

   > Sir Anthony Absolute/Mrs Malaprop
   > Bob Acres/Sir Lucius O'Trigger
   > Lydia Languish/Julia Melville
   > Jack Absolute/Faulkland

5. Write about Mrs Malaprop's misapplied words and what they signify with regard to her character.

6. What difficulties or opportunities can you perceive in a stage production of *The Rivals*? Give specific examples from the text.

7. Is Fag a well-written part?

8. '*The Rivals* is a first rate Comedy of Manners.' Explain this statement and say how far you agree with it.

9. Describe the relationship between Jack and his father *or* between Julia and Faulkland.

10. '*The Rivals* is a very funny play. Some scenes are hilarious.' Do you agree with this comment?

FURTHER READING

The text
C. J. L. Price, ed., Sheridan, Richard Brinsley: *The Rivals*, included in The Dramatic Works of Richard Brinsley Sheridan (Clarendon Press, Oxford: 2 vols, 1973)
Elizabeth Duthie, ed., *The Rivals* (New Mermaids, Ernest Benn Ltd, 1979). The footnotes and page by page glossary are valuable aids to study.

Correspondence
C. J. L. Price, ed., *The Letters of Richard Brinsley Sheridan*, vol. I (Clarendon Press, Oxford: 1966)

Biography
Moore, Thomas, *Memoirs of the Life of the Right Honourable Richard Brinsley Sheridan* (1825; 5th edition, 2 vols, 1927). A fine and entertaining work by a younger contemporary.
Darlington, W. A., *Sheridan* (Published for the British Council in pamphlet form by Longmans, Green & Co., 1951). A brief account of the life and work by a dramatic critic.
Bingham, Madeleine, *Sheridan – The Track of a Comet* (George Allen & Unwin, London: 1972). Modern and thorough.

Criticism
Loftis, John, *Sheridan and the Drama of Georgian England* (Basil Blackwell, 1976). A fine study of the whole subject.
Leech, Clifford and Craik, T. W. (general eds), *The Revels History of Drama in English*, vol. 6: 1750–1880 (London: 1975). Helpful to students at all levels.

Background Information
Plumb, J. H., *England in the Eighteenth Century* (The Pelican History of England, vol 7. orig. 1950).

Smollett, Tobias; *The Expedition of Humphry Clinker* (1771). A most enjoyable Bath novel. Good companion reading for *The Rivals*.

Miscellaneous
Palmer, D. J. (ed.), *Comedy: Developments in Criticism* (Casebook Series, Macmillan, 1984). Great thinkers on what makes us laugh.

Mastering English Literature
Richard Gill

Mastering English Literature will help readers both to enjoy English Literature and to be successful in 'O' levels, 'A' levels and other public exams. It is an introduction to the study of poetry, novels and drama which helps the reader in four ways - by providing ways of approaching literature, by giving examples and practice exercises, by offering hints on how to write about literature, and by the author's own evident enthusiasm for the subject. With extracts from more than 200 texts, this is an enjoyable account of how to get the maximum satisfaction out of reading, whether it be for formal examinations or simply for pleasure.

Work Out English Literature ('A' level)
S.H. Burton

This book familiarises 'A' level English Literature candidates with every kind of test which they are likely to encounter. Suggested answers are worked out step by step and accompanied by full author's commentary. The book helps students to clarify their aims and establish techniques and standards so that they can make appropriate responses to similar questions when the examination pressures are on. It opens up fresh ways of looking at the full range of set texts, authors and critical judgements and motivates students to know more of these matters.

THE MACMILLAN SHAKESPEARE

General Editor: PETER HOLLINDALE
Advisory Editor: PHILIP BROCKBANK

The Macmillan Shakespeare features:
* clear and uncluttered texts with modernised punctuation and spelling wherever possible;
* full explanatory notes printed on the page facing the relevant text for ease of reference;
* stimulating introductions which concentrate on content, dramatic effect, character and imagery, rather than mere dates and sources.

Above all, The Macmillan Shakespeare treats each play as a work for the theatre which can also be enjoyed on the page.

CORIOLANUS
Editor: Tony Parr

THE WINTER'S TALE
Editor: Christopher Parry

MUCH ADO ABOUT NOTHING
Editor: Jan McKeith

RICHARD II
Editor: Richard Adams

RICHARD III
Editor: Richard Adams

HENRY IV, PART I
Editor: Peter Hollindale

HENRY IV, PART II
Editor: Tony Parr

HENRY V
Editor: Brian Phythian

AS YOU LIKE IT
Editor: Peter Hollindale

A MIDSUMMER NIGHT'S DREAM
Editor: Norman Sanders

THE MERCHANT OF VENICE
Editor: Christopher Parry

THE TAMING OF THE SHREW
Editor: Robin Hood

TWELFTH NIGHT
Editor: E. A. J. Honigmann

THE TEMPEST
Editor: A. C. Spearing

ROMEO AND JULIET
Editor: James Gibson

JULIUS CAESAR
Editor: D. R. Elloway

MACBETH
Editor: D. R. Elloway

HAMLET
Editor: Nigel Alexander

ANTONY AND CLEOPATRA
Editors: Jan McKeith and
Richard Adams

OTHELLO
Editors: Celia Hilton and R. T. Jones

KING LEAR
Editor: Philip Edwards

Also from Macmillan

CASEBOOK SERIES

The Macmillan *Casebook* series brings together the best of modern criticism with a selection of early reviews and comments. Each Casebook charts the development of opinion on a play, poem, or novel, or on a literary genre, from its first appearance to the present day.

GENERAL THEMES

COMEDY: DEVELOPMENTS IN CRITICISM
D. J. Palmer

DRAMA CRITICISM: DEVELOPMENTS SINCE IBSEN
A. J. Hinchliffe

THE ENGLISH NOVEL: DEVELOPMENTS IN CRITICISM SINCE HENRY JAMES
Stephen Hazell

THE LANGUAGE OF LITERATURE
N. Page

THE PASTORAL MODE
Bryan Loughrey

THE ROMANTIC IMAGINATION
J. S. Hill

TRAGEDY: DEVELOPMENTS IN CRITICISM
R. P. Draper

POETRY

WILLIAM BLAKE: SONGS OF INNOCENCE AND EXPERIENCE
Margaret Bottrall

BROWNING: MEN AND WOMEN AND OTHER POEMS
J. R. Watson

BYRON: CHILDE HAROLD'S PILGRIMAGE AND DON JUAN
John Jump

CHAUCER: THE CANTERBURY TALES
J. J. Anderson

COLERIDGE: THE ANCIENT MARINER AND OTHER POEMS
A. R. Jones and W. Tydeman

DONNE: SONGS AND SONETS
Julian Lovelock

T. S. ELIOT: FOUR QUARTETS
Bernard Bergonzi

T. S. ELIOT: PRUFROCK, GERONTION, ASH WEDNESDAY AND OTHER POEMS
B. C. Southam

T. S. ELIOT: THE WASTELAND
C. B. Cox and A. J. Hinchliffe

ELIZABETHAN POETRY: LYRICAL AND NARRATIVE
Gerald Hammond

THOMAS HARDY: POEMS
J. Gibson and T. Johnson

GERALD MANLEY HOPKINS: POEMS
Margaret Bottrall

KEATS: ODES
G. S. Fraser

KEATS: THE NARRATIVE POEMS
J. S. Hill

MARVELL: POEMS
Arthur Pollard

THE METAPHYSICAL POETS
Gerald Hammond

MILTON: PARADISE LOST
A. E. Dyson and Julian Lovelock

POETRY OF THE FIRST WORLD
WAR
Dominic Hibberd

ALEXANDER POPE: THE RAPE OF
THE LOCK
John Dixon Hunt

SHELLEY: SHORTER POEMS &
LYRICS
Patrick Swinden

SPENSER: THE FAERIE QUEEN
Peter Bayley

TENNYSON: IN MEMORIAM
John Dixon Hunt

THIRTIES POETS: 'THE AUDEN
GROUP'
Ronald Carter

WORDSWORTH: LYRICAL
BALLADS
A. R. Jones and W. Tydeman

WORDSWORTH: THE PRELUDE
W. J. Harvey and R. Gravil

W. B. YEATS: POEMS 1919–1935
E. Cullingford

W. B. YEATS: LAST POEMS
Jon Stallworthy

THE NOVEL AND PROSE

JANE AUSTEN: EMMA
David Lodge

JANE AUSTEN: NORTHANGER
ABBEY AND PERSUASION
B. C. Southam

JANE AUSTEN: SENSE AND
SENSIBILITY, PRIDE AND
PREJUDICE AND MANSFIELD
PARK
B. C. Southam

CHARLOTTE BRONTË: JANE EYRE
AND VILLETTE
Miriam Allott

EMILY BRONTË: WUTHERING
HEIGHTS
Miriam Allott

BUNYAN: THE PILGRIM'S
PROGRESS
R. Sharrock

CONRAD: HEART OF DARKNESS,
NOSTROMO AND UNDER
WESTERN EYES
C. B. Cox

CONRAD: THE SECRET AGENT
Ian Watt

CHARLES DICKENS: BLEAK
HOUSE
A. E. Dyson

CHARLES DICKENS: DOMBEY
AND SON AND LITTLE DORRITT
Alan Shelston

CHARLES DICKENS: HARD TIMES,
GREAT EXPECTATIONS AND OUR
MUTUAL FRIEND
N. Page

GEORGE ELIOT: MIDDLEMARCH
Patrick Swinden

GEORGE ELIOT: THE MILL ON
THE FLOSS AND SILAS MARNER
R. P. Draper

HENRY FIELDING: TOM JONES
Neil Compton

E. M. FORSTER: A PASSAGE TO
INDIA
Malcolm Bradbury

HARDY: THE TRAGIC NOVELS
R. P. Draper

HENRY JAMES: WASHINGTON
SQUARE AND THE PORTRAIT OF
A LADY
Alan Shelston

JAMES JOYCE: DUBLINERS AND A
PORTRAIT OF THE ARTIST AS A
YOUNG MAN
Morris Beja

D. H. LAWRENCE: THE RAINBOW
AND WOMEN IN LOVE
Colin Clarke

D. H. LAWRENCE: SONS AND
LOVERS
Gamini Salgado

SWIFT: GULLIVER'S TRAVELS
Richard Gravil

THACKERAY: VANITY FAIR
Arthur Pollard

TROLLOPE: THE BARSETSHIRE
NOVELS
T. Bareham

VIRGINIA WOOLF: TO THE
LIGHTHOUSE
Morris Beja

DRAMA

CONGREVE: COMEDIES
Patrick Lyons

T. S. ELIOT: PLAYS
Arnold P. Hinchliffe

JONSON: EVERY MAN IN HIS
HUMOUR AND THE ALCHEMIST
R. V. Holdsworth

JONSON: VOLPONE
J. A. Barish

MARLOWE: DR FAUSTUS
John Jump

MARLOWE: TAMBURLAINE,
EDWARD II AND THE JEW OF
MALTA
John Russell Brown

MEDIEVAL ENGLISH DRAMA
Peter Happé

O'CASEY: JUNO AND THE
PAYCOCK, THE PLOUGH AND THE
STARS AND THE SHADOW OF A
GUNMAN
R. Ayling

JOHN OSBORNE: LOOK BACK IN
ANGER
John Russell Taylor

WEBSTER: THE WHITE DEVIL AND
THE DUCHESS OF MALFI
R. V. Holdsworth

WILDE: COMEDIES
W. Tydeman

SHAKESPEARE

SHAKESPEARE: ANTONY AND
CLEOPATRA
John Russell Brown

SHAKESPEARE: CORIOLANUS
B. A. Brockman

SHAKESPEARE: HAMLET
John Jump

SHAKESPEARE: HENRY IV PARTS
I AND II
G. K. Hunter

SHAKESPEARE: HENRY V
Michael Quinn

SHAKESPEARE: JULIUS CAESAR
Peter Ure

SHAKESPEARE: KING LEAR
Frank Kermode

SHAKESPEARE: MACBETH
John Wain

SHAKESPEARE: MEASURE FOR
MEASURE
G. K. Stead

SHAKESPEARE: THE MERCHANT
OF VENICE
John Wilders

SHAKESPEARE: A MIDSUMMER
NIGHT'S DREAM
A. W. Price

SHAKESPEARE: MUCH ADO
ABOUT NOTHING AND AS YOU
LIKE IT
John Russell Brown

SHAKESPEARE: OTHELLO
John Wain

SHAKESPEARE: RICHARD II
N. Brooke

SHAKESPEARE: THE SONNETS
Peter Jones

SHAKESPEARE: THE TEMPEST
D. J. Palmer

SHAKESPEARE: TROILUS AND
CRESSIDA
Priscilla Martin

SHAKESPEARE: TWELFTH NIGHT
D. J. Palmer

SHAKESPEARE: THE WINTER'S
TALE
Kenneth Muir